"There's a great deal to b
you hope to spend a life
Really knowing him, that i
stands for. Believing in hi
for good.

"On the day of our baptism, every one of us declared that we accepted our Lord Jesus Christ as God and Savior. Most of us said this through our godparents. This is the faith that made Christians of us—that made us members of Christ in his one, holy, catholic and apostolic Church.

"The big question is this: Do we really believe it *now*? Do we mean it with all our strength? We'd like to believe it, yes, but perhaps we don't know enough about our Lord to 'go all out' for him. That is why really getting to know him is something that should make a tremendous difference in our lives."

This is the opening page of *Christ the Lord* and is typical of the direct and simple approach to God which Fr. Sloyan offers his readers. He is eminently qualified to write a work of this nature since he is Chairman of the Department of Religious Education at the Catholic University of America in Washington, D.C. In addition Fr. Sloyan is a frequent contributor to many major religious and educational journals, and has served as a parish priest in the Trenton Diocese.

CHRIST THE LORD

GERARD S. SLOYAN

ECHO BOOKS

A Division of Doubleday & Company, Inc.
Garden City, New York

Echo Books edition published March, 1965
by special arrangement with Herder and Herder, Inc.

Grateful acknowledgment is made to Hi-Time Publishers, Inc., for permission to reproduce the copyrighted material contained in this book; to Atheneum Publishers, for the quotation from Ignazio Silone's *Fontamara;* to Duckworth Ltd., for Hilaire Belloc's *Sonnets and Verse;* to The Macmillan Co., for Eileen Duggan's *Poems;* to The Bruce Publishing Co., for *The New Testament* translated by James Kleist and Joseph Lilly; and to the St. Anthony Guild Press for *The Holy Bible* in the translation made for the episcopal committee on The Confraternity of Christian Doctrine by members of The Catholic Biblical Association of America. The poem on page 83ff is from *The Eagle's Word* © 1961 by Gerald Vann, O.P., and reprinted by permission of Harcourt, Brace & World, Inc.

Nihil Obstat: John T. McGinn, C.S.P., Censor Deputatus
Imprimatur: Patrick A. O'Boyle, Archbishop of Washington
June 19, 1962

Printed in the United States of America

EPISCOPO CLEROQUE TRENTONENSI
FRATRIBUS MEIS

CONTENTS

INTRODUCTION

It takes a certain foolhardiness bordering on insensibility to attempt again what the four evangelists have done so well. To bring alive on the printed page the Jesus of Nazareth whom Christians venerate as the world's Savior and whom countless others consider one of the wisest and holiest of men is to court failure. Yet it is common to those who believe in any person or cause to give testimony to their faith. Friends everywhere speak enthusiastically of friends. When the faith concerned has a more than natural quality, when the partner in friendship is someone believed in as true God and true man, the likelihood of written testimony to this faith and love does not diminish but rather increases. It is, in other words, entirely to be expected that Christians should write about Christ.

The chapters that follow are in that long-standing tradition. They do not comprise a "life of Christ" in the classic sense, the kind of thing that began with the 14th century Carthusian Ludolf of Coblenz and has culminated in modern works such as those of Lagrange and Prat. The chapters are much more like the gospels themselves from which they derive, being a series of thematic considerations based solidly on the existing faith of the Church in Jesus Christ. Many important pieces of gospel witness are absent from these pages: the narrative of Zachary's vision in the Temple, with which redemptive history proper begins; the story of the man born blind; the Transfiguration. If any principle of selection is at work here it is an attempt to feature aspects of the Lord's saving ministry that are less familiar to many. These outlines for consideration are supplementary, above all. The faith of

Catholics and of many other Christians in the full divinity of Jesus Christ is clear and strong; their supernatural belief in his full human status is often not so firm. There is a general understanding that "Jesus was a Jew"; the actual implications of his relation to his people Israel have never been brought home to large numbers. That the eucharist is the food of Christians, and that the Church is Christ's mystical body, all know; how, exactly, they stand in relation to Christ in glory, who will return to raise them up at the Last Day in virtue of the eucharists they have received in the Church, many have not pondered on. It is to provide the opportunity to learn or to recall such truths that this modest volume exists.

The speech employed is the language of every day. The examples, one hopes, are commonplaces of modern life. Occasional resort to levity, however painful to the discriminating reader, is an attempt to levitate the spirit and not to debase the message. St. Augustine, after all, demands *hilaritas* as the condition of instructing in Christ. The word had a slightly different meaning in the Fifth century but it connoted "cheerfulness," at the very least.

The deep-seated wish of the writer is that he will create in the reader a threefold sense of dissatisfaction: at his own imperfect familiarity with the New Testament, at the writer's bumbling attempts to direct him to the riches that are there, and with life generally—which is to describe that hunger and thirst for holiness which will have its fill only when Christ the Lord returns and "is all, in all."

THE AUTHOR

CHRIST THE LORD

–1–

THE JESUS WHOM THE FIRST BELIEVERS PREACHED

There's a great deal to be said for knowing Jesus Christ if you hope to spend a lifetime calling yourself a *Christ*ian. *Really* knowing him, that is. Knowing who he is and what he stands for. Believing in him–throwing in your lot with him for good.

On the day of our baptism, every one of us declared that we accepted our Lord Jesus Christ as God and Savior. Most of us said this through our godparents. This is the faith that made Christians of us–that made us members of Christ in his one, holy, catholic and apostolic Church.

The big question is this: Do we really believe it *now*? Do we mean it with all our strength? We'd like to believe it, yes, but perhaps we don't know enough about our Lord to "go all out" for him. That is why really getting to know him is something that should make a tremendous difference in our lives.

Most of us have no time for fakes or frauds, people who sail under false colors. The most obvious types are the professional "con men." At the amateur level you have the athlete who shaves points in a basketball game for a gambling syndicate's cash.

Most of us, however, get caught up in the more ordinary kinds of fakery. We copy homework like crazy, or fill out padded expense accounts.

Do you remember the knife-like words our Lord threw at the phonies he met? You will find them in chapter 23 of Saint Matthew's Gospel.

There is still another way of playing the fraud. Most of us were born into a community of people who believe in Christ –our family, our parish, our neighborhood. We said we were *Catholic* because everyone else said we were. It did not take much thought or effort.

Once in awhile we thought about it a little, about what it meant to be a Christian—when we made our first communion or came to love someone who was not a Catholic and didn't bother about church. Perhaps then we thought a little harder about the big difference between *saying* we were a Catholic and *being* one.

Sometimes it seems that the more we learn about Jesus Christ, the less we know him. What sort of person was he? If he was truly the Son of God in human flesh, how could anyone stand having him for a daily acquaintance? or having him as an enemy—that's even harder to understand. So *getting to know him* may be the trouble.

It could be that we are bothered by the idea of what Christ is supposed to mean to us *now,* granted all that the Bible and the Church say about him is true. To some of us, Christ may seem too "far away and long ago." In church we are told that he is the *central figure* in our lives and in history. But when we walk downtown on Saturday night, in the parks, past the cheap movie theaters and the "gin mills" we think, "Who's kidding who?"

The best way to get facts is to go back to sources. What did our Lord's first followers think about him? To find that, we go to a book in the Bible called "The Acts of the Apostles." Saint Luke wrote it some time after the year 65 A.D. Its first part tells the way the disciples preached about Jesus around the year 30, when he arose from the dead and went back to his Father. When we read Acts we learn what Christ meant to those men and women who were willing to suffer for him. We need to have him mean that much to us now!

Those first disciples felt terribly close to Christ—and to one another. Why? Because the Holy Spirit had let them know exactly who their great teacher was. During his lifetime they never did get the point entirely—but later they did. And then, instead of wanting high places in Jesus' kingdom, their only boast was that they were disciples of Jesus of Nazareth. Why were they his followers, his friends? Because of what they *knew* about him. He was not merely their friend; he was the *Lord!* (For the Israelites—or *Jews,* as they were later called—only God was "the Lord").

How could these strict Jews say that about a *man?* Because the Holy Spirit had assured them that Jesus, whom wicked men had killed, and who rose again from the tomb, was "Lord." Men had no other savior but him. To believe in him was to have life. (Jesus said that, himself. See John 6:47). So nothing that the mobs or rulers did could shake them or weaken their faith in him.

What about us? Can we take it—the jibes, the sneers sometimes—and remain loyal and unshaken?

Most of the ideas we need to grasp about Jesus are in that story of the strong, courageous faith of the early Church in Jerusalem that we find in Acts. In the first place, without faith we cannot be sure who Jesus is. Saint Paul tells us we can't even say his name, except in the Spirit. (I Corinthians 12:3) That means if we want to understand Jesus we have to ask God the Holy Spirit, the third person of the blessed Trinity, to make our personal Pentecost—our confirmation—mean something to us.

Then we have to *know* Christ as his disciples did. They had their warm memories of him. We can "read all about it" in the New Testament. They knew him in the breaking of the bread—we can know him in the eucharist.

Going all out for Jesus means loyalty. And *loyalty to Christ means the cross!* It is strange, but the cross won't bring only misery. It will bring a sense of security in life, and purpose—yes, it will bring *real* joy—not just a wandering about aimlessly, looking for random kicks, but a sense of deep-down, lasting happiness. For the worst that *can* happen, *has* happened. CHRIST WAS CRUCIFIED! And Christ won the victory! He is in the glory of the Father. If we stay faithful to him, the glory that is his will be ours too.

There is *one condition* that cannot escape our notice when we read the Book of Acts: *If we don't spread the good news about Christ's victory over death and sin, it soon stops meaning much to us.*

No wonder we feel a little rocky about the whole business of who, exactly, Jesus is. We don't pray enough—to the Holy Spirit for light and guidance. We don't read enough—of God's love for us in the Bible. We twentieth century disciples don't fulfill our duty of confirmation enough—by telling the good news to others.

Lots of communions received, did somebody say? Good, wonderful—but *that is not enough.* Look at Acts 2:42 and you'll see that that's only part of it.

–2–

THE BAPTIST'S CRY: JESUS TESTED IN THE DESERT

Have you ever heard about whole towns putting on "Pioneer Days" pageants? Usually the men have to grow beards and carry flintlock muskets. The women make their own pinafores and dustcaps. Why all this? Because we have a romantic idea that our people were braver and more resourceful in the old days. When the wagon trains went west, everything was different—we like to think.

It is much the same with religious groups. Most of the small Christian churches that are called "sects" have this mark in common: they want to capture the simplicity of the early days of the Church. They read the Bible with great care, especially the *Acts of the Apostles* and the letters of Saint Paul. Then they try to copy the smallest details they read about. They want to live *exactly* as the New Testament says the first Christians lived. No changes; no developments; everything just as it was centuries ago.

Well, the people of God in the Old Testament, his beloved people who called themselves "Israel" (at that time they weren't known as "the Jews"—that came much later), thought in pretty much the same pattern. They made a romantic ideal out of their own early history. For them, nothing had ever been quite the same since their wanderings in the desert, back in Moses' time.

In those days, according to the writing of Ezechiel, one of their great teachers, God had come upon Israel. She was like an abandoned, newborn child. First, God raised her. Then he showered all kinds of gifts upon her. Then he took her as his own bride! This is a poetic way of speaking, of course, but it helps us to understand. If we think of Israel as the bride of God, it is easier for us to learn what Jesus meant in many of the things he said. The love between God and Israel was so strong in the early desert days that Israel, like a bride, endured hardships that she has never been able to put up with since. At least, that is the way people liked to remember it.

The place where all these memories centered was the desert. This *desert* does not mean the broad sands to the east of Israel's homeland, stretching out toward the River Euphrates, in what is today called Iraq. It was not the kind of Foreign Legion desert that makes us think of palm trees and camels. No, it was a narrow little neck of land to the south and west of them, which joined Asia to Africa. Today there is a canal on the part that is closer to Africa, the Suez Canal, near Egypt. "East of Suez"—you may be familiar with that phrase. Well, the land *immediately* east of Suez is a rocky peninsula called *Sinai,* where it's impossible to live. It was grim—it *is* grim. Something like Alcatraz, only miles and miles of it.

When Israel (the people of God, the bride) was in this rocky desert, the people grumbled terribly. They wanted to be back in pagan Egypt, where at least the water was fit to drink and they could eat meat regularly. Then God put their faith to the test at the rock where Moses struck his rod. Israel failed the test miserably!

Even then, God's love for his people would not let them down. Food fell from heaven—manna. There were quail. The people's worn clothes and battered footwear became like new. And for all of God's goodness to Israel, what did she do in return? The Israelites turned against the Lord, their strong lover; they turned against his servant, Moses, and made idols to worship. In general, the Israelites couldn't get off that rocky Sinai peninsula fast enough!

It's funny what changes the years will bring! The boy who used to whine about the cold water in the tub grows up to be the man who is forever praising its good influence on his character. In the same way, Israel centered all her loving memories on that desert stay of "forty years." The only way she could ever be "saved," that is, rebuilt as a people of God, was by acting out again her whole history as a people. She would be tested again as once she had been in the desert, but this time she would pass the test. She would cross over the Jordan River—as she did years ago under Joshua—and come up out of the water of this same stream into the "promised land"—the "kingdom of God."

Do you have the picture? Can you see now why John the Baptist had gone into the desert? John had everyone talking. For he went into the wasteland, dressed like the prophets of old, eating the same wild food. Why? Because the Lord would begin the work of saving his people *in the desert.* (The men of Judea who have left us the "Dead Sea scrolls" fled from the cities and towns of their time to live in the desert—for the same reason as John's).

Then a call came from God to John the Baptist, a call that came to no one else. John was to preach to all the people sorrow for sin and a complete change of heart—and he did. He gave them an *outward* sign, too, which showed that they meant to change *inwardly.* He led them into the Jordan where they were covered by the waters—and they came up out of the river, ready to hear about a new life in the "kingdom of God."

That is what John prophesied was coming upon them. He taught that the eighteen centuries of longing—since Abraham's time—were shortly to come to an end. And thousands of people believed him. It is more correct to say that the people believed God, and were convinced that John was a true prophet speaking in his name. (Mark 1:1–8)

And then came Jesus: at first only an onlooker at the edge of the crowd. He had come to begin the work his Father sent him to do. Jesus came up to John, who recognized him and did *not* want to give him the sign of sorrow for sin—the waters of the Jordan. But Jesus insisted. "And the heavens were torn apart" at the moment Jesus came up out of the water. The dove, a sign of God's Holy Spirit, hovered low over the waters, just as had happened at the creation of the world. The voice of God the Father was heard: "This is my Son, my beloved. My favor rests on him." (Mark 1:9–12)

Then Jesus was sent into the desert by the Spirit, where he put man's enemy, Satan, to flight by succeeding in the three tests where his people, Israel, had failed. He won a smashing victory in all three encounters because his trust was wholly in his Father.

You can look all of this up for yourself. First, read Saint Matthew's Gospel, starting with chapter 4. Then turn back to the Old Testament, to Deuteronomy 8:3 for Jesus' first answer; to 6:16 for his second; his third answer is found in 6:13.

It is sometimes difficult to understand fully what our Savior said and did. Often it takes study, chiefly study of the Old Testament. One may even say that Jesus cannot be known—let alone loved and followed—unless we picture him as someone at the very end of a long story of God's love for men: the climax, the greatest gift.

One wonderful thing about the Bible is that you can find your own life story in it. It is the story of every man's life in miniature. The Old Testament is a story of growing up from infancy with never-ending favors done by a loving parent—and endless acts of ingratitude by a fickle and ungrateful people who take the parent for granted. The New Testament is an image of what we ought to be—ourselves at our potential best—just as Christ and the Church he founded is the people of God at its best.

We are called *to be Christ,* in fact. That is the whole meaning of our baptism.

Our Jordan was the font in which we were baptized. The "land of promise" we are walking about in now is the Church, for God does not plan to give men any higher or better life on earth than life in the Church. For you, the question is: Has Satan challenged *you* in the desert yet? Not by little, everyday temptations that we can charge to weak nature, but by big ones—the kind that Israel and our Lord both endured. The temptation to pride, the temptation to satisfy every desire you experience. The temptation to trust in yourself, and not in God.

You, since your baptism and confirmation, are God's beloved on whom his Spirit has descended. Are you well into your public life? What are you doing, for your part, to help save the world?

–3–

JESUS CALLS HIS DISCIPLES

Leadership is a funny thing. It's like charm in a woman, as Sir James M. Barrie says in one of his plays, *What Every Woman Knows:* you either have it, or you don't.

Some leaders show no air of self-importance—others are full of vanity. There are bullies among the leader class—and gentlemen. There are strong men—and cowards. Some attract all men equally—others make their point with a small "in-group" and through them influence others. Many of this second type are despised by the non-leaders, *but they follow them, all the same.*

Jesus was in that select group of persons who could have a few intimate friends—say fifteen or so—yet never lose his personal appeal to thousands. Even now, you don't feel that *you* cannot be close to Jesus because John was such a good friend of his. The special relation of Jesus with Peter does not seem to interfere in the least with his relation to *me.*

Do you see what we're getting at? It's hard to define, but you meet a few persons in life who have this same gift. They seem to be able to *give themselves completely* to a *limitless number* of individuals—and not only while they are talking to them!

What we have just said seems to describe *friendship* as well as it does *leadership.* That's because a leader is a friend at his best. The fine feature about it is, there are certain areas—the things you are interested in, for example—where *he* follows *you.*

When we read the gospels with care, we immediately see something of the magnetic quality of Jesus' personality. It's true that he acquired a good number of close friends who had been ready-formed in piety by John the Baptist. These friends took religion seriously, eight or ten of them at least. They really cared! When John turned them over to Jesus they went to him direct. This gives us a good clue to the character of Jesus! Although at the moment he was an unknown, these new-found friends followed him immediately.

Remember, Jesus wasn't even from Judea, and it's hard to imagine the contempt the sophisticated people from the south (Judea) had for the bashful bumpkins (the "hicks") of the north (Galilee). We have grown used to the idea that Jesus is of the tribe of Juda and the house of David. We are also likely to think that all pious Jews at the time of Christ were clear as to where the Messia was to come from. Not at all! There were all sorts of conflicting theories. The most commonly held was the "house of David" theory, for the people thought he had to be a king. Down along the Dead Sea, however, the monks of Qumrân were expecting a "Messia of Israel and Aaron" (two!).

Some of the priests thought he had to be the son of a priest (which Jesus wasn't). And to imagine that a descendant of David would successfully re-establish the throne—well, that was as much expected from Galilee as that the next president of the United States will be a Mississippi Negro. "Study the Scriptures and you will find that prophets do not come from Galilee." (John 7:52) That was a well-known gibe, a bit of contempt, which the Jerusalem leaders hurled at the Galileans. Most of the twelve men Jesus chose as his apostles were from Galilee. Yet, that did not keep Nathanael from wise-cracking, "Can any good come from Nazareth?"

New friends of the Nazarene left their families and their careers to follow him! The only adequate explanation of this fact is the personal pull which Jesus exerted on them. They were really drawn to this man!

In the first place, he was mysterious. There was so much you couldn't know about him. What could be known was admirable, but there was so much more *to* this teacher! And no one could see it all on one visit, the way it had been with the Baptist. John dressed like a prophet, he ate like one, and his message was very close to that of an Isaia or a Jeremia. To hear him was to recognize his type immediately.

Jesus was different. He was a quiet type; not mousy, just quiet. An ordinary town-dweller, he wore the clothes of his time. He had no special badges of discipleship, no "campaign buttons" to give out, such as long fasts or assigned daily prayers. All Jesus did was look a man in the eye. If he thought he had the goods, he said, "Follow me." That didn't mean, "Walk this way." It meant, "Be of my company—ten, twenty years, a lifetime!" Jesus let them know that the reign of God they all awaited had arrived—and was somehow centered on him.

When these people quit their work to follow Jesus, they weren't thinking of God's glory entirely. They meant to be right there when the major plums were given out. After all, he did choose twelve—and Israel had twelve tribes. They put two and two together and got *twelve:* jeweled thrones (they thought) on which they hoped to sit and judge their own people. Nice, high-minded motives!

You know what they got. Nights out under the stars without even a *foxhole.* (Funny that the bloody business of war should steal a term from the gospel of peace!) They walked forever, and they policed huge crowds, and they went hungry. He promised them even more when he asked, "Can you be drenched in the bath of suffering that I will be drenched in?" They said yes—and when they said it they probably meant it. (See Mark 10:38; Matthew 20:20–23).

John, in the fourth gospel, is interesting when he tells how Jesus first called his disciples. It's at the end of the first chapter—but he skips all around Jesus' public career to make his point. First, the Baptist calls him "the lamb of God"—a title for the Messia in popular religious writing of that time. (See what wonderful use the Apocalypse makes of it, from 5:7 to the end of chapter 7). Andrew then calls him "Messia." Philip adds "the one spoken of by Moses in the Law and by the prophets." (Dt. 18; Is. 53) Nathanael reaches the climax: "Son of God," he says, "King of Israel." (Read John 1:36, 41, 45, 49).

Then Jesus answers this great litany of faith in him by naming the title he liked best of all, the one he gave so much meaning to: "Son of Man." (John 1:51)

You ask, what can this possibly mean to *me*? If you've been baptized—and confirmed—you might as well know the box you're in. "Can you be drenched in the bath of suffering that I will be drenched in?" he asks you! The trouble is, some of you have begun to realize all that he expects of you. You may not like it. Cheer up. You can run. (Three of his bravest did, in the garden). You can sell out. (No need to name the poor fool who did that "because he was a thief," John 12:6).

The plan to stick with Jesus has a good deal in its favor. "No man ever spoke as this man speaks," the crowds said. And they were right. Listen to him—just once! If all that he did were to be set down in detail, it's doubtful the whole world could hold the books that would need to be written—this is the thought that concludes the four gospels.

There is an even better reason for staying with him. You may not see heaven wide open, and angels going up and coming down upon the Son of Man. But you'll gain a friend in him, at a time when you may need one desperately. Then a funny thing happens. You gain a whole lot more friends. People begin to look more and more like him.

It's no use to push this. You have to find out for yourself if it's true, or just something the four evangelists made up.

–4–

THE FIRST OF JESUS' SIGNS

Why did Almighty God send his Son to us? God's reason for sending Jesus to us was that he wanted to speak to us.

God had spoken to his beloved people Israel many times before: through the forefathers of the nation—Abraham, Isaac and Jacob; through the great prophets, starting with Moses. After the prophets, he sent men of wisdom to speak a word of love to his people. These men wrote great religious songs like the psalms, and many wise sayings by which God hoped to make Israel a holy nation.

But the last and greatest Word he spoke to his people was his own Son—a Word clothed in the fullness of manhood—as the last gospel of the Mass says: "The Word was made flesh."

We men have any number of ways in which we can get ideas across to one another. Spoken words are surely the commonest way. Written language comes high on the list. But even before writing, there is the gesture, the *sign*. A shrug, a rolling of the eyes, a finger drawn across the throat, can speak volumes. If there is some circumstance where we can't speak (like being behind the wings during a play), we act the whole thing out so as to get our meaning across. Have you ever seen someone go through a set of gestures which say, "Run upstairs and get the dishes for the second act"?

There is a game played with signs where you act something out in brief sketches to get your meaning across. You know it—it's called *charades*. Perhaps you've seen it played on television where, unfortunately, it isn't played very well. There, it's pretty much a case of making syllables with one's hands, the way deaf people do in sign language.

In a really clever game of charades, someone who is a good actor and has a quick mind does an entire short play, without words, to get across a book title or a witty saying. In this, husbands and wives should not be on opposite sides because they know each other's thoughts too well. Their minds work together and so it's a giveaway.

In Old Testament times, the prophets used to act things out that way in order to teach the people. Sometimes they would use an object, like an almond tree or a frying pan or a clay pot. That seems strange to us. If we had something to say to thousands of people, we'd print it in the newspapers or go on television. We would say it directly, so that no one would miss our meaning. The Israelites were different. They liked to speak with their hands and with their whole bodies. Above all, they liked to speak in *signs,* almost in riddles, to get their most important messages across.

Are you getting the picture? And do you suppose that Jesus our Lord, who was the greatest of the prophets ("Nay, and more than a prophet," he once said of himself), would speak to God's people in a way entirely different than they were used to? Of course he wouldn't. Jesus worked signs to convey his meaning—just as did all those men before him whom God had sent with messages to the people.

Jesus spoke to his fellow Jews in a language of gesture which they understood as well as they did their own Aramaic speech. They knew very well what his signs *stood for*—oh, maybe not always right away, but after they had thought about them. They understood because they had nearly two thousand years of memories to draw on.

There is really little need to review the details of the first *sign* Christ worked at Cana, near his home town of Nazareth. You have been hearing of the miracle of the water-made-wine ever since you started going to Mass. Why did Jesus do it, besides wanting to show his power as the Son of God? He had several reasons: one, to do a kindness for the family that was embarrassed; then, to teach us something about the power of his mother's influence with him—that he finds it difficult or impossible to refuse a request from her; also, he wanted to teach his mother that she had to give him up now, to do his great work. But the real reason he worked the sign at Cana is more important than all of these!

Remember, Jesus worked this first sign at a wedding, or rather at the great feast of celebration that followed a wedding. The water Jesus changed was not just any water. It was found in *six* water jars (not *seven*, Israel's sacred number like the *Sabbath*—the seventh day—meaning the holiness of God). No, there were *six* jars—one short of perfection.

The water was there for the guests to wash their grimy hands, and their feet, dusty from the roads, before they dared to eat. This was part of strict religious custom, according to the Pharisees. So you see, the water jars were a *sign* of Israel's religion. They stood for the Law of Moses, as it was interpreted by the rabbis of Jesus' time.

When Christ changed the water into wine, therefore, he didn't only work a great miracle. He performed a *sign* that could have had a great deal of meaning for the onlookers, especially if they were looking for the "kingdom of God"—as we know his newly made fishermen friends were. Right before their eyes they saw the Law (the water) give way to the new teaching that he would give them (the fiery red wine). It was like saying outright that Christ considered himself superior to Moses, the great lawgiver.

Then remember, it took place at a wedding feast! Every pious Israelite knew that the wedding feast was the sign of a final union in love between God and his people. Israel was like his virgin bride. (Remember, we talked about the "bride" before, in an earlier chapter?) And when *this* great marriage banquet was celebrated, that would be the last age of the world.

Long after the miracle had taken place, Jesus' disciples turned over in their minds every word of his, every glance. Was this, they wanted to know, the coming of God's kingdom in glory? It was—and at the same time it was not. "My hour has not yet come," he said quietly. Later, he would suffer for men's sins and be glorified. That would be his "hour."

But this day at Cana was indeed the beginning of the

"last times." He was, after all, Israel's Messia, the only Son of his Father, come to save all men. He let his mother and his new friends know this by working a sign—a sign that meant that the long-expected "kingdom of God" had arrived.

Can we be sure of all this? It may seem like reading an awful lot into the story. Not really. It's only seeing in the story all that's there. Saint John gives us the clue by his solemn and mysterious ending: "This first of his signs Jesus did in Cana of Galilee. By it he revealed his glory and led his disciples to believe in him."

Those disciples didn't believe that Christ could work miracles—for they *saw* the miracle, and you don't believe what you *see*. No, what they began to *believe* in was his *glory*—and this, for the reporter John, meant his being glorified by his Father as the chief figure of the Last Days on the earth.

Israel's long awaited wedding feast (the sign of God's union in love with his people) had really begun in the person of this Jesus of Nazareth.

Some of you who read these lines are married, and many will be. We could of course speak of that in connection with Cana. But this first of Jesus' signs was not worked for *some* of his followers, but for *all* of his followers.

What one meaning does it have for all of us? Chiefly this: *to believe in Christ is to let yourself be changed totally by God.*

Read that prayer in the offertory of the Mass, the one the priest says over the water as he pours a few drops into the wine. It's all about changing us into God, just as the Son of God was changed into one of us. What it means is that the eucharist can make an entirely new person out of us!

Have you ever thought of that? That at the Mass it is not only the bread and wine that is changed—but, most of all, *you yourself?* That means that every Mass is Cana—a happy feast between God and his people as bridegroom and bride.

All this the gospel is trying to say to us—if only we will let it.

–5–
JESUS CASTS OUT DEMONS

You might be surprised to learn how much Jesus had to do with the devils of hell! You might, that is, if you're not in the habit of reading the four gospels.

Open your New Testament to the Gospel according to Saint Mark—the second of the four gospels and the shortest one. The first half of it might almost be called a book about "casting out devils." Mark sometimes calls them "demons"—but more often his term for them is "unclean spirits."

It is important for us to know what place these terribly unhappy creatures hold in our belief as Christians. Nowadays very few moderns except Christians—and not all Christians, at that—believe that there are any such thing as devils.

You will learn, if you haven't already heard it, that most modern people are satisfied that what used to be called "possession by demons" was really epilepsy or some serious mental illness. People were just ignorant in ancient times, the moderns say. The people in biblical times did not know how to explain all the strange behavior of sick people. Because they could not account for it otherwise, they blamed it on "devils"—that's what the moderns charge.

That is one way to be wrong about demons: to disbelieve in them entirely. The other way—and this is just as much opposed to the faith of the Church—is to believe too much in devils. This usually takes the form of telling stories about "possession" which are like glorified ghost stories. In a way—though the teller usually doesn't know this—multiplying these tales takes for granted that Christ hasn't really broken the power of Satan by his death and resurrection.

You remember the task we set ourselves at the beginning of this book, don't you? We said we would look into those events in Jesus' life that were especially important to him, and to the disciples who wrote about him. These are the things that have to be important to us—even though we haven't heard of them before, even though they sound a bit queer the first time we do hear of them.

That portion of the gospels about demons is extremely important. We *must* understand it if we are to get the full message of the Master about the work he came to do.

Jesus, you see, is holiness itself. In the gospels, that is the clearest fact about him. He is holy with the holiness of God!

Now, ever since the people we call Israel had known their God (and the "Lord"—which was their special name for him —was a holy God from the very first), they'd had some idea of the opposite to holiness: a terrifying, dark someone whom the Bible calls "the adversary." The Hebrew word is "Satan" —a creature who is "set against" God.

The first parts of the Bible to be written are not clear on him at all. All sorts of vague and uncertain statements are made in the earliest portions of Scripture about the force of evil. What *does* become clearer and clearer, as the Bible period continues, is that evil isn't only a *thing*, it is a *person*. Rather, it is persons without number, who once were with God, but who now are against him.

All this supposedly happened long before there were any men on the earth. The first one to make clear what happened between God and the angels was the Christian author of the Book of the Apocalypse (the last book in the Bible). He tells, in his chapter 12, about a mighty struggle in heaven between the archangel Michael, and the proud angel "Satan or the devil" and his disobedient followers. "This is the hour of victory for our God, of his power and royal rule, when his Christ wins the mastery, for the accuser of our brothers has been hurled down, he who accused them before our God day and night." (Apocalypse 12:10)

In our Lord's time, even though the Bible hadn't much to say about devils, the common people lived in deadly fear of them. When Jesus came, he made it his business to set them free from many fears and superstitions. Every word he spoke removed another burden that their religion teachers had put on their backs.

Jesus would say, "This is what the Scriptures say . . . but this is what I say." What *he* said was what the Scriptures really meant. The Scriptures had always meant love and obedience, never a set of back-breaking rules and regulations. It is strange, but that is what the rabbis of Jesus' time had made of the Law which was given to their fathers out of love on Mount Sinai.

For all these reasons you might expect Jesus to say, if it were true: "The Scriptures seem to be describing certain evil spirits who hate God and hate men. Actually, though, this is just a manner of speaking. Like so many of the 'traditions' of the Pharisees, this idea of devils is only a human invention that has grown beyond all bounds. There aren't any devils: that's just a way of describing ignorance and fear and superstition."

Did Jesus say that? He said nothing of the sort. He dealt with some of the sick whom he cured as if they were precisely that: sick men. With others, he acted quite differently. He did not speak directly to the sick person, but to other individuals, to wicked spirits who were dwelling inside the sick. Jesus never stopped to argue with these unclean spirits. He simply commanded them to go, and to leave the sick person in peace.

When Jesus spoke to the demons, Israel had its first absolute certainty that evil was real in the person of fallen angels.

That may sound strange to us, but it is quite true. Remember, the people of God were uncertain about a great number of things until God's own Son came to earth. If you read about the sin of Adam and Eve in the garden (chapters 2 and 3 in Genesis), you will see that evil is described there under the form of a snake—the great sign, for ancient Israel, of heathen religion, that is, all that is opposed to God.

This uncertainty about who or what evil, or the evil one, was, continues all through the holy books. You find "Satan" mentioned—in the book of Job and in the prophet Zacharia, *but only Jesus settles the problem finally.* He is the first one to give us complete certainty about the devil.

God has an ancient enemy, Jesus teaches us, who is also man's enemy. The "Son of Man," as our Lord loved to call himself, comes from heaven to break the power of this evil one. The very first service he does is to *identify* him. The devil really *is.* Let there be no mistake about that!

Secondly, the devil's hold over men is broken because he cannot accept the fact, he cannot stand it, that one of these men, one of these creatures whom he despises, is holiness itself! "What have we to do with you!" they shriek. They call him "the holy one of God"—a truth that not even people of good will were yet able to say about him. Jesus' tone is firm—and final. "Go out of him!"

Really, it's great to see what Jesus thinks of Satan. He calls him a liar (remember the lie the serpent told Eve?) and a murderer (recall the story of Cain?) from the beginning. Jesus has no fear of the devil, nor respect for him. He despises him. Once when dozens of his disciples returned to him in high spirits, after casting out demons in his name, Jesus said, "Yes, I was watching Satan fall, like lightning out of the sky." (Luke 10:18)

When we pray the great prayer of Christ's saving death on Good Friday, we say a wonderful thing. We rejoice: "He has broken the serpent's tooth of hell!"

How about you? What does it all mean to you? Perhaps you recall your first experience of evil, and it made you sick. We don't mean by committing evil—that's too awful to think of; but the shocking mystery of deep hatred or disregard for God!

Have you run into that yet? It can take any number of forms, like the dirty-picture industry: those people who make millions by trying to destroy the image of God that exists in man. They turn man into not just an animal but into something that is a mockery of human or animal existence.

Something else you may have known at first hand is slow,

burning jealousy: the kind that destroys everything it touches. Another face of evil is hatred between two persons who would rid the earth of each other if they thought they could. They're too superstitious, or too afraid of punishment, to kill —so they just hate.

Maybe what's bothering you is a bad habit that *looks* like evil. It has an ugly face, and it's all around you. You've tried everything you could to be rid of it, but it keeps cropping up again no matter what you do. You may be tempted at times to lose hope. You say, "I don't need any explanation about the devil. He seems to be everywhere I turn."

That is why it is important to know what the gospels tell us about Jesus and the demons. *He has defeated them, smashed their offensive—right, left and center!*

What's important to keep in mind is that, ever since our baptism, Satan has been put to flight before us. Jesus lives in us. Every time we take holy water we recall that we have been made new in Jesus Christ. "If God is with us, who can be against us?" Saint Paul asks.

Be fearful about the power of evil to destroy us, yes, but most of all, have an utter contempt for it, because the great gift Jesus brought us was the forgiveness of sin. Satan is finished—*kaput*—all washed up! Christ conquers! Christ rules! Christ is in command!

–6–

JESUS RETURNS TO NAZARETH

One of the hardest things about growing up is that not everybody does it at the same time. (If they did, that would make matters even worse!) As it is, young people don't seem to know how their parents think. And this is every bit as true in reverse: parents would take a rocket trip to the moon if they thought they could find out there how their children think.

When you get right down to it, the big gap in life is not so much between youth and middle age, as between two quite different ways of looking at things. Just glance around you and see if that isn't so.

A quick glance at the "laws of the heart," and you see how true it is that age doesn't really make the big division in life. It isn't money, either, or brains. The real difference is a matter of "outlook," for lack of a better word: our way of thinking about God, and other people, and the world in general.

Doesn't it seem to you that people who think exactly as you do are fairly few? You *seem* to be on the same wave length as dozens of others. But deep down inside you, if you'll admit the truth, you know that there are only about half a dozen persons in the world who seem to understand you.

Because this business of understanding one another is so vital, it's a comfort to know that, when God's Son became man, he had the same problem as everybody else. Jesus had it much more, in fact, because his idea of what the savior of the world should be (the only right idea on this subject) and everyone else's idea were a world apart. You may say that the reason Jesus came to earth was to make his idea of "salvation" everyone else's.

At the start, very few people knew what Christ meant when he said that God's kingdom had already come. In particular, his own family members did not understand him; and that is a hard fact for *us* to understand.

The gospels give the names of four of Christ's kinsmen ("brothers" is the ancient name for close relatives). They are called James and Joses, Simon and Jude. There are women cousins in the family, too, but we don't have their names.

We don't suppose it's true of all of them, but some at least had no sympathy whatever for this "odd" cousin of theirs. Even poor Mary, his mother, who loved and trusted him perfectly, is dragged along with them. Women in those days didn't assert their rights the way they do now. Mary was probably just glad to get a look at this good son of hers—whom she wasn't seeing much of any more.

When Jesus came home to his own town of Nazareth things reached the worst pass of all. His own townsmen tried to take his life! He managed to escape them, though. Unbelievable, did you say? No, not really. You see, Jesus had a bad habit of telling the whole truth to people at the time they were worst prepared to take it in. It was always the right time, of course. Jesus was no fool, and he was never merely argumentative. When he argued, his arguments were always based on his thoughts, never on his temper or his prejudices. And he sailed right in! Good grief (as Charlie Brown would say), but he had nerve!

He paid the price, of course. Everybody who has both brains and guts pays the price. What we mean to say is, "they get you in the end." That isn't just being cynical but factual. They do—the *they* being people who have neither brains *nor* guts, or one but not the other. If, besides these two qualities of intelligence and nerve, you have goodness as well (when you're good all the time and on principle we call it "virtue")—the opposition is just *sure* to get you somehow.

Jesus had the keenest human intelligence God ever gave a man. He had a nerve like steel, and holiness higher than that of all the saints and angels together. Notice how we keep speaking of his human qualities. That is most important.

Even though Christ is God's only Son and in every sense

equal to the Father, it is through his holy manhood that he saves us. Don't ever lose sight of that great Catholic truth. It is all too easy to do just that. He wouldn't have all those human gifts *unless* he were the Son of God. But because he has them, we call him brother, and savior, and Lord.

That's what makes everything easier. When your own older brother has been through every suffering before you—suffering which you are enduring now; when you know how much more he had to take than you, because he was so much holier and brighter than the people who couldn't understand him—then you can put up with a lot!

This is especially true when your own family doesn't understand you. We're not talking, for the moment, about all those thousands of selfish people who want to have everything in life their own way. We're talking about those cases where a person wants to be a perfect disciple of Christ, wants to *go all out* for him—but the people he lives with daily don't seem to have any idea of what he is getting at. The cases that are sadder still are those where family or friends *do* know, *are* aware—and oppose this kind of life bitterly.

Making fun of the other fellow is the big weapon of hurt pride. "Who does she think she is, running off to Mass all the time!" That's known as the gentle-sneer approach. Another is the deep-dig-direct: "I may not be much on religion because I'm earning food and clothes for the lot of you. But believe me, my religion is as good as yours, and if you ask me a damn' sight better." Fact is you hadn't asked him. He's very dear to you. You had just hoped with all your strength that he would understand the ideals you're trying to live by.

"So he came to Nazareth, where he had been brought up," Saint Luke writes. (4:16) First, he went to the synagogue on the Sabbath, as he regularly did. Nothing new about that. Then he asked the man in charge of the service to hand him the scroll. Again, nothing new. He read from the prophet Isaia, chapter 61, at the beginning of the chapter.

It was all about someone whom the Lord would anoint with oil, so that he could spread the good news to the poor—those depressed and deprived people who had no earthly hope in this world. This "someone" on whom the Spirit of the Lord rested was going to let the prisoners out of jails, give sight back to the blind, and let the broken victims of tyrants go free.

"I am that man," said Jesus. "This text has come true in your hearing this day."

Well, they all hoped that "someone" would make Isaia's prophecy come true. Jesus was a local boy: "the carpenter's son," they called him. Their first feeling was one of surprise—not anger. *What, then, turned them against him?* As we've said before, he sailed right into them. He reminded them that being a Nazarene was nothing; indeed, being an Israelite was nothing. *What really mattered was the free choice of a holy God.*

Jesus told them a couple of stories to make his point—stories about the days of the prophets Elia and Elisha. In both stories, God worked wonders not for Israelites but for Gentiles: people from Phoenicia (the widow of Sarepta, whose son the Lord restored to life) and from Syria (the general of the king's army, Naaman). Our Lord's point is that God helps *whom* he wants to *when* he wants to. No one can say, "That isn't fair," because *he* is the Lord.

In the same way, Jesus said, Nazareth shouldn't expect to see him work the miracles he had done in the neighboring towns, on some sort of "native-son" principle. God is not committed to geography, nor to home ties, nor to Jewish blood. He is absolutely supreme over everyone and everything, and he is a holy Lord.

And there, it seems, is where most of the trouble lies when you try to follow Christ very closely. The first thing you know, you're not doing what everyone else on the block is doing. You become different! And being different is the one "sin" people can't stand: not being a carbon copy of themselves.

The next step after that is, you're supposed to consider yourself *better* than everyone else. You never said that for a minute. You never thought it, in fact. They say it.

What can you do about it? Probably nothing. Like Jesus himself, you have to follow your clear call from God—and take your lumps.

It would be pleasant to report that, after a while, everyone will begin to understand you, and to love you. Some will. Not all, though. In fact, not many.

But Jesus didn't let rebuffs from his neighbors and townsmen bother him too much. He didn't let wise cracks or the opinions of men stand in the way of his carrying out the great mission God had sent him to earth to accomplish. He kept right on doing his Father's will. So should you, so should we all!

–7–
THE ENEMIES OF JESUS

The four gospels are filled with mysteries. In the last chapter we were speaking about Jesus' being rejected by his own family and townspeople. Before that we dwelt on the dark mystery of evil, especially as it is reflected in the evil wills of the "unclean spirits"—the devils of hell.

But perhaps the most mysterious thing of all about the earthly life of Jesus is the way it ended, and why it ended as it did. Not even his closest friends were prepared for that. If we were to read the gospels for the first time, without knowing their ending, it is very unlikely that we would be prepared for the climax.

It was God's will, of course, that Jesus should die for the sins of men. Now, no human mind can fathom the depths of God's love for us and all that he means to do out of that love. It will always remain a mystery why Christ died—it's as mysterious as God himself. But at still another level, the level of human motives and the like, the violent end of Jesus is almost an equally great mystery.

Consider this: Jesus was an extremely popular person. Despite the fickleness of all crowds everywhere, he could not have lost his hold on the people completely in a matter of weeks or days. The common people listened to him willingly, the gospel says. (See John 7:31). They marveled at him at every turn. "No one ever spoke the way this man speaks." (John 7:46) He was not accepted at home by his own people, it is true (Mark 6:5–6), but strangers thought he was great!

The reason for this popularity? Christ represented for them a hope they had never had before. He told them they were worth something. These poor, "marginal" farmers who could scarcely raise enough food to eat, these day-laborers with crooked backs who hadn't a single decent day in prospect this side of the grave, began to think that maybe life had some meaning for them after all.

It wasn't that he promised them riches, or even freedom, the way a modern leader of downtrodden peoples might do. He didn't seem to care a fig for economics or politics as solutions to their problems. All he cared about was these people *as persons:* the poor. And they cared for him in return *so much* that the four gospel writers could scarcely express it in words. Some of the popular demonstration of affection was selfish and self-seeking, but much of it was genuine.

Another thing that kept happening—in a way it *had* to happen—was that Jesus told the crowds they hadn't much to hope for from their religious leaders. You see, he was terribly interested in religion as something of the *head* and *heart*, but the religious leaders of that time were strong for it as a thing of *prestige* and *pocketbook*. They were not only doing *good* at religion; they were doing *well*. The leader class was riding high. Jesus represented a popular threat to them on two fronts: that of *power*, and that of *income*.

Those are the two threats no dictator can stand. That is why Castro in Cuba, or Kadar in Hungary, or name-your-strongman always tries to put religion out of business. First he tries to make it work for *him*. (The Chinese "People's Republic" is playing it that way; so is the Communist régime in Poland). When this doesn't work, the dictator moves in. He shuts the churches, closes the schools, seizes the properties. *The one thing he can't stand is opposition.* When he can't *buy* the opposition, he *crushes* it.

It isn't always the case that religion is the *victim*, however. Sometimes religion itself is the *dictator*, and ordinary people are the victims.

In our Lord's time it was *official* religion that couldn't stand the opposition of real religion which Jesus represented. It tried to silence the voice of the greatest of God's spokesmen, his Son. Because the leader class in official religious circles couldn't silence him, it turned murderer like Cain.

But the blood of Jesus cried out from the ground, like innocent Abel's. Cain's question had been, "Am I my brother's keeper?" (Genesis 4:9) The high priests and the scholarly "doctors of the Law" decided that their answer to this question should be "No." Or rather, after keeping a good eye out for themselves, they chose to be the keeper of every Jewish brother they had—except Jesus of Nazareth. They said, "It is better that one man should die [that a little blood should flow, in other words] than that the Romans should come and take away our holy place and our nation." They made it a clear choice between the temple area in Jerusalem and the power they wielded within it, and a just man. Justice lost!

Oh, they might have carried on at the temple with Jesus the victor over them, but they had the grim prospect of seeing their revenues shrinking to almost nothing. After all, hadn't he said once that the time would come when people wouldn't worship in Jerusalem any more, but "in spirit and in truth?" (John 4:24) What's the "percentage" in a religion like that? the leaders figured.

The other thing that infuriated them was that Jesus, in his talks to the crowds, spoke of the leaders' evil lives, and they knew it. He made fun of their spirit of unbearable self-importance. He described them as a pit of snakes; as the filthy, buggy underside of a stinking tomb. (See Matthew 23: 33, 27).

There's a lesson for you in how to lose friends and alienate people! Jesus didn't care a bit. He had come to bear witness to the truth and he couldn't rest until the job was done. His enemies—the rich and powerful elements in organized religion —were ready to murder him after his first few public talks, but they knew they had to go slowly, slowly, for fear of the crowds. The crowds had a sort of natural instinct for the truth, and when they came face to face with truth in the form of a Man, many of them threw in their lot with him for good. (John 7:40) "I will follow you wherever you go" (Luke 9:57), one man said.

The priests and the lawyers didn't dare finish him off early and so they watched—and waited. The man of passion will kill in a blind rage. The cool, crafty hater takes his time. He can wait. When the enemies of Jesus thought they had waited long enough, they sprang. (Matthew 26:3–5) Being natural cowards, of course, they used the services of one of his friends as an informer. (Vv. 14–16)

Nowadays we talk about "insecurity" quite a bit. The court psychiatrist will prove how this man steals cars and that one molests girls because neither was brought up properly. The offender had parents who neglected him or helped warp his character. They never made him feel sure of himself in a normal human way, and so he took steps on his own. He went to great lengths of crime or violence to prove that as an individual in his own right he could *do* things, like anyone else.

There seems to be quite a lot to this theory. You've known some pretty warped characters in your day, haven't you? What their trouble frequently seems to come down to is *insecurity*. It is fairly clear that the Jerusalem gang of bully-boys had a bad case of it. They were not on God's side because their prayer lives had dried up long ago. Their temple-sacrifices had become empty ritual, strictly a matter of profit and loss.

The Old Testament prayers called the psalms say that a good man's strength is the Lord. All his security should be in him. But that was far from the case with the priests and the scribes and their different hangers-on. They trusted chiefly in the coin of the realm. Another thing that gave them a feeling of security was pride of ancestry: descent from Abraham, Isaac and Jacob, from Moses and all the prophets (whom their forefathers had murdered, as Jesus somewhat tactlessly reminded them). In a word, they were insecure because they didn't possess the living God—only toys and trinkets, like money and the blood of Abraham. (See John 8:33).

When Jesus came along he threatened it all, and they panicked. He not only made them quake at the thought of losing their own spot in the local universe, he let them know that *true religion was about to be shared with the Gentiles.* For eighteen centuries, God had performed his mighty acts in the midst of his own people—tiny Israel, his chosen. The Lord God began to say through Jesus his beloved Son that her uniqueness of privilege was at an end.

The prophet Isaia had promised it, and now it was coming true: the *new temple* was to be a house of God *for all peoples.* (Isaia 56:7) A *new sacrifice* would be offered from this time forward, not just in Jerusalem, but from sunrise to sunset throughout the world. (Malachia 1:11) *A new creation,* a royal race of priests from every nation under heaven, would do in spirit (that means, taken at its fullest, in the Holy Spirit) what the sons of Levi did in the blood of goats and heifers.

In a word, the true religion was branching out. It was going to have a place *for all men of good will* everywhere. It was going to have no place whatever for the greedy power élite, into whose hands it had fallen as almost a private possession. As Jesus put it in one of his stories, the owner of the vineyard was going to come and take the property away and put it in other, worthier hands. (Matthew 21:41)

That is the way things are from now until the end, when Jesus returns in the glory. Christianity means bigness, broadness; no frontiers of the mind or of the human spirit. To be the enemy of Christ means to have a heart full of barriers. Really, the correct spelling is "barrier$," for that's the highest one of all.

–8–

THE FRIENDS OF JESUS

The proverb says, "You can choose your friends, but you can't choose your relations."

Choosing our friends is an important part of growing up. If we are truly mature, no matter what our age, we tend to select as friends people who will bring out the best in us. When young people tag along with a fast crowd (they like to think they're *with* them because they're wanted, but it's really "tagging along"), parents begin to get nervous. It isn't only that they panic at the thought of drag-strips, or cruising around all night whistling at girls. (Dressing to be whistled at?) That *does* give parents something to think about, but those bits of foolish behavior are only symptoms of a deeper-lying condition known as "immaturity."

There should be no misunderstanding here. Losing one's life in a highway crash or forfeiting one's chastity isn't to be dismissed airily as "only a symptom." Each has something pretty final about it. But *the state of mind that leads up to these tragedies,* or any other you may care to name, *is the underlying cause of them.* If the Christian can be rid of that state of mind (or avoid ever acquiring it), then *life will be a simpler, happier business all around.*

Getting to be mature is the remedy for immaturity. The pattern of our friendships is both the sign that maturity is taking place and the best guarantee that it will take place. If that sounds like a roundabout sentence, it's because the whole thing is a roundabout process. Our friends help us to grow up; yet we pick good friends only if we're already in the process of growing up.

Sometimes we pick friends who don't look like such a good

bet to help anybody—themselves or us—but they turn out to be good friends and good for all concerned. Why so?

Well, because we figured things out right; because we could see good qualities in them that others couldn't pick out, qualities that perhaps hadn't begun to develop much yet. We made an act of faith in them as possible good friends, and by the very confidence we showed, we helped bring about a change in them. It also proved to be a good thing for us, this business of working to bring about a change.

Let's give a look at the pattern of friendships in Jesus' life. We have to start by recognizing how mature he was from the beginning. It isn't just that Christ was a man of thirty-odd years when we first meet him. He was fully mature in ways that a great many people of that age are not. Self-composed, thoughtful, prayerful; "outgoing," extremely interested in the well-being of others—all these things Jesus of Nazareth was. They add up to being mentally and emotionally mature.

Notice in the gospels how much respect he shows for everyone he meets. There is one great exception: he is blistering with phonies and frauds! With everyone else he is fairly stern —or serious, if *stern* is too strong a word. *But he meets them on a man-to-man basis that is calculated to bring out the best that is in them.*

Take, for example, the fishermen whom he recruits as his disciples early. They aren't pious types by Pharisee standards or the standards of the scribes—those members of the Pharisee party who knew the Scriptures inside out. Look at Simon and his brother Andrew, and the other brother-combination, James and John: none of the four could be called "learned in the Law." But they were pious in another way, in that they "looked for the kingdom of God."

There was a good bit of self-seeking in it. They hoped that Israel would triumph over all her enemies, and that they would be there for the final "kill," so to say. Still, they had left much behind them to follow the preaching of John the Baptist. He was down along the Jordan's banks in Judea, to the south, whereas their home place was to the north by almost a hundred mountainy miles.

That switch couldn't have been easy, especially when what awaited them at the end of their journey was a good, stiff going-over by John, a man who preached a hard life and a total change of outlook. Jesus picked them as his friends because they were already men of action and men of decision who had a basically religious view of life.

They were a pretty immature crowd, though. Petty, that is to say. You remember Nathanael's famous sneer, "Can anything good come from Nazareth?" He himself was probably from Cana, just a few miles away. *Big* deal! It was all Squaresville, Galilee, no matter how you looked at it, but Jesus paid no attention to this provincialism of the mind. He was fishing for men who would really mature and amount to something, and he knew he had come across a few good types.

Sometimes they nearly drove Christ crazy with their bickering and their self-interest. He came down from the mountain where his face and his whole body had shone for a brief moment with heavenly glory, and he ran into a lack of faith in his own friends that prevented the Father from working a cure. (Mark 9:14–29) Even on the home stretch—on their way to Jerusalem to see him suffer and die—two of them began a silly, schoolboy quarrel over who would sit on his right hand and who on his left in "the kindgom." (Mark 10:35–40)

This underlines the fact that we all encounter curious weak spots in the character of even the best of our friends. We then have to decide whether they are worthy of our continuing friendship. If they are, why we keep on working at helping them to mature. Quite unlike Jesus, we are helped to become more complete human beings by helping them. It is a mutual self-help process.

This doesn't mean that we have "snobbism" as a goal. It just points out the fact that friendship is a very special thing that needs to be worked at hard. Having everyone as a brother in

Christ is a goal for all of us. To make friends of a special few, though, is a life work for everyone.

The unique thing about our Lord is that he can make a special, close friend out of millions and millions of people who have been baptized into him. No one else can do that. That is because no one has a heart with the capacity his has.

The other type of person that "the carpenter, the son of Mary" (Mark 6:3) attracted to himself was the rag, tag and bobtail sort that didn't make the social register. The Samaritan woman at Jacob's well embarrassed the disciples into silence when they came back from buying food in Sichar. (John 4:27) They got her number fast. There were tight-fisted tax collectors ("gougers," actually, not professional men who did a professional job; see Luke 5:29–32). There were people who hadn't been to synagogue service or to the temple for a pilgrimage feast for years. (John 7:49) Then there were the people of thoroughly mixed up lives who had got themselves in the mess of making a living from the mystery of sex. (Luke 7:36–39)

The men of Jesus' day who were officially "good"—who swung morality about like a club, rather than held it in awe for the gift of God that it was—couldn't understand how Jesus could make friends from people such as these. Their trouble was, they didn't know what holiness meant. Therefore, they couldn't see how he, who was all-holy, could purify those he came close to *just by being near them,* if only they would let it happen.

Perhaps that is the one thing we need to know most about the friendship of Jesus: it can burn away our sins and our shortcomings completely, it can change us into different persons—if we'll let it.

The things that discourage most of us aren't the sins of the "sinners" in the gospel. They may not even be the sins that every normal person is supposed to know all about and be troubled by. All right, so much the better for us. But every single one of us does want to throw in the sponge at some time or other because of sheer discouragement at being weak, or unimportant, or just "no good."

That's the time to remember that *our real importance lies outside ourselves.* We are holy because Someone who is holy loves us, and the love he bears us makes a change in us. In other words, because we have a friend in Jesus, nothing need ever be quite the same again. We can even come to experience a strength and holiness in ourselves by which we are able to be of help to others who are weak.

They badly need the friendship of Jesus Christ. *Will you bring it to them?*

THE MOTHER OF JESUS

It is part of Catholic faith to honor Mary as the mother of God. It is part of Catholic piety to hail her as the holiest of the saints of the Most High. She is our chief friend and helper in that heavenly company. As Queen of Heaven, she is high above the angels, too.

There is no belief about the Virgin Mother that is not very much a part of our belief about her Son. The "mystery of Christ" includes the mystery of Mary. That means that, in God's plan to save us, Mary has no independent place. She is forever someone who has meaning only in light of the work of her Son, Jesus, as our high priest. He is the one and only person who acts as a link between God and the human race. His mother is never far from him as he fulfills his unique role.

Jesus Christ is the great offerer of himself, whole and entire, to God. Mary, however, is the one who provided him with his human frame and form. Therefore, it is right to say that much of what he gives to God as our priest he got from God through her.

Mary also is a "giver," along with Jesus, in the sense that his self-giving (or "sacrifice") is the model for hers and our complete giving over of self to God. No one—absolutely no one—can be in the intimate personal relation with Jesus that each of us is called to, without patterning himself on Mary, the first believer. He alone is the way, but she directs us in following along this way. If we do follow, then what is offered to God is not Jesus only but "the whole Christ," he and we together.

A little instruction on the mother of Jesus seems necessary because we daily come across such soupy—and downright questionable—teaching about her in Catholic writing. There come to mind immediately several devotional journals on our Lady that enter Catholic homes, only because the publishers managed to get the householders' names and won't "let up." The difficulty is that, while Mary is always presented in them in a mother-and-son relationship, she seldom appears in the context of the whole mystery of our redemption.

It is God the Father who saves us through his Son, in unity of the Holy Spirit. In this work of God, the three are inseparably one. They are the great God who saves. They cannot have a human creature allied with them, so to say, in this work of saving men—except the one human creature that stands in a unique and special relation to the second person, or Son, whom we call the Word. *That creature is the human body and soul of Jesus.*

Now, the body and soul of Mary, despite the closeness in words and deeds and mannerisms to her Son, is not something that can be identified by nature with the work of God to save us. No, our Lady is forever aligned with us, because she is forever a creature of God who needs saving like everybody else.

Another way to put this is to say that God is joined to no human creature so closely as he is to the body and soul of Christ in the mystery we call the "incarnation." (That word means simply, "taking human nature").

But—and this is a big and important *but*—of all the cases where God has come especially close to creatures by showing his choice and affection for them, he has never come closer to anyone than to Mary. Sometimes, because of her part in the mystery of the incarnation, we call her the daughter of the Father, the mother of the Son and the bride of the Holy Spirit. That is surely a correct way to speak of Mary.

The same cannot be said of any other Christian. Yet, of each one of us, it can and must be said that, at our baptism, we came into a distinct relation of love with each of the three persons in God. In the case of no two human beings is that relationship identical. Just as you and your brother or sister mean something different to each of your parents (and they to you)—though there's love in all directions—so you stand in a relation to Father, Son and Spirit that is *like* our Lady's, but *by no means the same* as hers.

What makes the difference? Two things: God's choice of her, and her response. First, he did not pick you out for the same role as Mary in the work of our salvation. She was given the more important task, you the lesser one. Yet if either you or Mary were to fail, it could be said that God's plan to save us had failed, in greater or lesser degree.

Second, given the fact of the difference in "vocations" (i.e., different work to do, different call from God), there is another major unlikeness between the mother of God and you. When we say "you," we mean everyone who ever lived, since no one has ever given so generous a "yes" to God as Mary since he began issuing calls to man to make man holy.

A vocation is a very common thing in life. Everyone has one. The call is not issued to each one of us to be a priest, the father of five, a day-laborer and an insurance salesman, all at the same time. The rule is, of course: different roles in the work of our salvation, different calls.

The four listed above are special vocations. The general vocation issued to all Christians—indeed to all men, if we carry out Christ's missionary command—is a call to holiness *in Christ*. The Father issues it. The Holy Spirit makes its acceptance possible. Every man is free not to answer it, but such a man is properly termed a fool if he understands it and turns his back on it.

How did Mary receive her vocation? You know the steps, surely. First, she was born into a holy nation, a priestly people. Then came the vocation to marry Joseph. After that, the angel's message, and with it, a call to two roles that seemed to cancel each other out—motherhood, and virginity. Mary couldn't understand this. No one can. But because it was God who issued the call, she said, "Let it be done." (Read Saint Luke's gospel, 1:26–38).

Her next call was to suffer deeply over the loss of her young Son. (Luke 2:41–52) When he grew up and left his home, going off to preach about his Father, he once told a crowd of people who had reported to him that his mother and his brothers were waiting outside, that doing his Father's will was a greater and more important thing than being related to Jesus. (Matthew 12:46–50)

On another occasion, Jesus had a perfect opportunity to join a woman in praise of his mother. Instead, he turned it into praise of anyone who heard the word of God and kept it. (Luke 11:27–28)

These references to Mary in the gospel are very puzzling to us. They certainly do fulfill, however, what the old man Simeon said would happen to her: "A sword shall pierce your own soul, so that the thoughts of many hearts may be revealed." (Luke 2:35)

If the normal human individual were asked what his biggest hardship in life was, he'd probably say, "Discouragement." That's the sword that pierces his heart. Friends and family don't seem to understand; one's work is hard; most boys don't make the teams they try out for; most girls can't manage to interest the one boy in the school they really want to like them. Result: *discouragement*. What is life all about? Almost everyone will tell you: "One big defeat, one setback after another!"

Ask Mary what life is about. She *really* knows. She'll tell you that it's one great mysterious plan of God to bring us to himself. Most of the time, she will say, he doesn't provide us with many clues. He is good at reminding us (as he reminded her) that sentiment doesn't come first, or even family ties.

Obedience is what matters: doing his will—which, incidentally, is by no means an easy thing to discover. He teaches us through setbacks much more than through easy victories. The goal is great, so the price is high. It was so with Mary, greatest of the saints. It is so with us.

"Behold your mother," Jesus said from the cross to his disciple. (John 19:27) Ask Mary, he is saying, the meaning of life. It is chiefly a plan, God's plan, framed out of love. If you do not come to believe that, life is almost unendurable.

THE STORIES JESUS TOLD

Abraham Lincoln was our great storytelling president. He'd had lots of experience as a backwoods boy, grocer's clerk, flatboat operator, lawyer, judge and Illinois politician. By the time he got to the White House, he seemed to have at his disposal ten thousand witty tales from his younger days, ready-made to suit the occasion.

It didn't matter if the point in question was the appointment of a federal judge, McClellan's skill as a general, or the financing of the Union Army. Lincoln always seemed to know some "character" from his Sangamon County days who once had an adventure that paralleled perfectly the issue under discussion.

"That reminds me of old Sim Cooley," the President would say, if the conversation got around to cheerful coincidences that were totally unplanned. "He said that the happiest man he ever knew in all southern Illinois was the fellow who managed to cut a bee tree down on his wife."

It is almost impossible to read about President Lincoln's yarns without being reminded of the parables of Jesus. Our Lord was just such a storyteller as that. His stories have passed the test of time much better, however. The chief reason for this, of course, is that he is the eternal Son of God, while Lincoln was a good man trying to serve God. Even so, Jesus wins out if you apply only the rules of good oral prose. His stories were better, even as stories.

Our Lord did not invent the form of storytelling that he used. He became the perfect master of a style that the rabbis (i.e., the teachers) of his own day employed all the time. They in turn got it from centuries of usage.

The Old Testament has a number of wonderful parables,

such as the story of the trees that chose a king, in the Book of Judges (9:7–21), or Nathan's tale about the rich man who, when he had a guest, robbed his own poor neighbor of his little ewe lamb. (II Kings 12:1–4) Look these stories up. You'll enjoy them. And if you have your Bible out, look up the ones in Ezechiel 17:22–24 and II Samuel (i.e., II Kings) 14:1–20, as well.

You will notice immediately that a parable is a story which makes some point about human behavior; in it, certain things are made to stand for other things. *Any tale, however brief, in which figures of speech are used, and one major comparison is identifiable throughout the telling, is a parable.*

Mashal is the way Jesus would have said the word for this kind of speech, in the Hebrew language. But, of course, the gospels were written in Greek, and our word *parable* is like the Greek word that was used for any *mashal* or comparison. The same Greek word was used by the gospel writers to describe a riddle, even though Hebrew has a different word for *that.*

We shouldn't say "any comparison" because there were certain types that our Lord never used. For example, he never employed a fable, the kind of story in which animals or trees are given the power of speech.

He never told a story about real people by name, a thing that Lincoln did *all the time.* There is only one proper name in all of Jesus' parables, that of the poor beggar Lazarus. But that was like calling him "Joe." It didn't mean a particular person at all.

Lastly—and this is very important—only very rarely did Jesus tell an allegory. *An allegory is that type of parallelism in which one person or thing represents another all through the story.* The best known of his allegory-parables is the one about the sower and his seed. Jesus goes on to explain it by saying that the seed is the word of God, and the path and the thorns and the birds are all the different states of the human heart as the word comes to it. (Read Matthew 13:4–9; 18–23)

That sower story is surely the best *known* allegory of Jesus. Yet the most important one is the story about the wicked men who killed all the collectors of rents for the vineyard, and finally the vineyard owner's son. Undoubtedly, Jesus meant to describe the stoning of all the prophets and lastly, his own destruction at the hands of the leaders of the people. He got his point across, all right, because this tale so infuriated his listeners that, after hearing it, they began their final plotting against his life. (Read Matthew 21:33–46).

It's pretty hard to get the full impact of our Lord's stories if we don't happen to be farmers (Mark 4:24–32) or fishermen. (Matthew 13:47f.) Probably an even worse handicap is not knowing how business transactions were carried on in his day (Luke 16:1–13; Matthew 20:1–16), or how cruelly desert chieftains—the gospel always calls them "kings"—dealt with their enemies and with their friends. (Luke 19:27) A few simple clues can help us, though.

Despite all the differences between his day and now, the rules for the human heart do not change. His parables of love and mercy are as easy to understand today as the day they were spoken.

The chief thing to remember is that most of the parables of Jesus have a single point. Look for *it*. Everything else in the way of detail is added just to make the story interesting.

Secondly, the king or the wealthy man must not be taken to stand for God the Father every time. Or, better, when he does stand for him, he does so in this way: that just as kings and grasping men can always be expected to act the way they do—cruelly, skin-flinty, taking revenge—so God can always be expected to be in fact the way he is—supremely just, forgetting nothing, kind.

A final important clue is that, when Jesus is talking about the "kingdom" that his people expected, he has the important task of correcting their many wrong notions about it. His big job is to make clear to them that being a son of Abraham or Israelite, or even being an observer of Moses' Law in full Pharisee style, will not do. God the Father has another set of qualifications, which Jesus has been sent to remind them of. These are *mercy* and *justice* (holiness)—and *sorrow for sin.*

That is why so many of our Lord's stories—all his "kingdom parables"—are Israelite-versus-Gentile stories. The laborers-in-the-vineyard is the best known of these. (Matthew 20:1–16) Who are the eleventh-hour crowd but Greeks and Samaritans and "sinners" of every kind, namely all others but the pious observants of the Law who think they have been out in the heat of the sun since Abraham's time.

The story of the wasteful son and the good boy who stayed at home is in exactly the same vein—Luke 15:11–32: "My son, you are always with me, and all that is mine is yours." So is the briefer story called "the parable of the two sons": "Son, go and work today in my vineyard." He answered, "I will not," but afterward he regretted it and went. The other answered, "I go, sir," but he did not go. Which of the two did the Father's will? (Read Matthew 21:28–32).

Earlier, we put the question of what the parables can mean to us. Well, we must get to know them, first of all. There are a good many more in the first three gospels than turn up in the various Sunday gospel readings. So comb your Matthew, Mark and Luke to discover the great variety of colorful tales that Jesus left behind him. Look especially in Matthew 13, then 18 to 25; Mark 4, and Luke 7 to 19.

Then see where it is possible that the story is being addressed to you. You may not know all the customs of those times, but you can see whether there is anything of the priest or levite on the Jericho road in you. (Luke 10:25–37)

Have you got as far as the wedding feast—the eucharistic table—without a wedding garment—a real spirit of faith, in eating the body of the Lord? (Read Matthew 22:12).

How does the Father "run out to meet you when you are as yet afar off"? (Luke 15:20) Have you ever really decided, with respect to life in Christ—the "kingdom of heaven"—that it is such a treasure that everything you own must be exchanged in order to come in possession of it? (Matthew 13:44–46)

There's one thing to remember about a teller of stories. He can always be dismissed by serious-minded types as a clown. Lincoln's enemies dismissed him that way. With Jesus' enemies, it was the same. "A spinner of yarns. Entertainment for the children. Who can be expected to listen to him?" they might have said.

Remember this: the world lives, not by its statesmen or treaties or battles, but by its stories. A simple tale can bear the weight of the profoundest truth man is able to bear.

Don't dismiss these parables by making the terrible mistake of thinking that you know them. All right, maybe you can finish five or six of them when someone starts one, just because you've heard it read so many times at Mass. Can you tell the one about the house built on sand? The rich man who was a fool? The king planning a war?

These stories won Jesus his best followers. They saved his life more than once. They earned him his fiercest opposition, and finally death. In twenty centuries, they have never faded from human memory.

What have you let them do for you lately?

arranged in order, in numbered groups [illegible] [illegible] they [illegible]

[illegible] Don't try to remember all that mass of stuff, the [illegible] can always be discussed [illegible] [illegible] [illegible] [illegible] [illegible] comes out and [illegible] that way [illegible] [illegible] [illegible] the same. A [illegible] [illegible] For [illegible] there [illegible] [illegible] can be [illegible] to them to [illegible] they might [illegible] still.

[illegible] [illegible] the world [illegible] and [illegible] [illegible] [illegible] battles [illegible] by [illegible] [illegible] the weight of [illegible] [illegible] that [illegible] [illegible] [illegible].

Don't dismiss [illegible] possible by making [illegible] [illegible] of [illegible] this [illegible] them [illegible] maybe you can [illegible] or [illegible] [illegible] [illegible] [illegible] once you've heard it said so many times [illegible] [illegible] all the [illegible] about [illegible] [illegible] [illegible] [illegible] you was a [illegible]. The king [illegible] [illegible].

These [illegible] [illegible] loyal followers. They [illegible] [illegible] more [illegible]. They [illegible] [illegible] [illegible] [illegible] and [illegible] [illegible] [illegible] [illegible] they have [illegible] from human memory.

What have you let them do to you, Stoll?

–11–

JESUS THE LAWGIVER

The Italian novelist Ignazio Silone writes about the poorest of the poor in the mountain towns of his own country. In one of his books entitled *Fontamara* he is describing the importance of lawsuits and the law in his area, which is not at all unlike the country in which Jesus Christ spent his earthly years.

"All the families," he writes, "even the poorest ones, have interests to divide among themselves, and if there are no goods to share, they share their misery. Therefore at Fontamara there is no family without some suit pending.

"As is known, the suits die down in the lean years, but they become bitter as soon as there is money with which to pay the lawyer. And there are always the same suits, unending lawsuits that are passed on from generation to generation in interminable hearings, eternal expenses, in blind inextinguishable bitterness—to establish the ownership of some thornbush grove. The grove may burn down, but the suit continues even more bitterly." (Dell Laurel edition, p. 17)

This fighting over an absolutely worthless piece of property gives us some idea of the misery of the very poor. But of course suing other people in court for no good reason is not confined to the poor. The rich do it too. In their case, it is a sign of something quite different: the unhappiness born of greed and of owning too much.

When you read the gospels you get some idea of this constant wrangling in the law courts we are speaking about. One day a man called to Jesus out of the crowd, "Master, tell my brother to divide the inheritance with me." (Luke 12:13) Jesus wouldn't have anything to do with the case. He told the man that no one had appointed him a judge over his claim—

even though, later, he was to say that he would be the judge of all men at the end of the world. (Matthew 25:31ff.)

Instead of giving an answer, he told a story about a grasping rich man who "couldn't take it with him." Read it in the twelfth chapter of Saint Luke's gospel. It's a great lesson on the folly of piling up too much cash.

In the middle of the Sermon on the Mount, Jesus refers to going to law over one article of clothing. (Matthew 5:40) Mind you, a shirt! And when he wants to tell people about the wrongness of most human anger—not just murder—the best way he can do it is to name two courts of law—the one in the local town, and the "supreme court" at Jerusalem—and finally the flames of Gehenna, the holy city's refuse dump, which signified punishment, by its fire.

All of the law courts the gospel speaks of were part of the religion of Israel. There was no such thing as what we would call a civil court. Religion governed the lives of the people in every aspect.

Whenever "lawyers" come up in the gospels, they are not very pleasant people. Almost always they are enemies of Jesus because he is a threat to their pretensions as "doctors of the Law" and "rabbis" (teachers). He blasts them once for a whole chapter's length. (Matthew 23) They are sometimes called "scribes"—like our word scribblers—because, in those days, to be skilled in reading and writing was to be concerned about the one great writing: Moses' Law.

Actually the Law was God's Law and Moses was only his scribe. Why, then, should Jesus, who always referred to God as "my Father," set himself against the writings that had come from heaven to men through the great lawgiver, Moses?

You can guess the answer to that one. He didn't. Never for a moment did our Lord take a position contrary to the writings of the Old Testament.

He was opposed only to the people who were making a fat source of income out of the Torah. Torah is the Hebrew word for Law. A better translation, perhaps, would be The

Instruction. Another abuse of the Law in those days was to employ it just to parade your knowledge.

Probably the worst abuse, though, was to think that your own human opinion of what it meant was more important than the words of the Law itself. Or going against its clear and direct meaning, and saying that some other complicated meaning—worked up by rabbis who were dead no more than one or two hundred years—was to be preferred.

All of these abuses were just ways of making religion serve men! And religion, of course, *true religion,* is the way man serves God.

The best statement we can make about Jesus and the Law is to say that he loved it and he kept it. Not a brush stroke, not the tiniest Hebrew letter—"i"—would go unfulfilled, Jesus said. The end of the world might be expected to come sooner. Read the verses near Matthew 5:18.

But the more we read the gospels, the clearer it becomes that Jesus means something quite different by "fullfilling the Law" than did the men of his time who were lawyers or scribes. The phrase, for them, meant keeping to some unimaginative, wooden sort of interpretation of a precept that had sprung up by human pedantry or genius. By "fulfillment," Jesus meant going to the heart of the meaning of a precept as it came from God.

For a young person to want to become a lawyer is a fine ambition. It is a higher ambition still to aspire to becoming a judge. A lawyer tries to get justice for his client but a judge, or court of judges, has the heavy task of deciding where justice lies in a particular case.

Only God knows the answer to that question in *every* case, but only the judge who fears God and loves his will can come close to being perfectly just all the time.

Everybody knows the jokes they tell about crooked lawyers. Sometimes they're not so funny, especially if your father or your brother is trying hard to be a good lawyer. These gags are especially unfunny to the family that has received an important, fair decision with the help of a lawyer, a man who has worked maybe years on the case. Ask a Negro American who is familiar with the NAACP how much justice his race has achieved through the law courts. Quite a lot, he'll tell you.

In the same way, we would make a terrible mistake if we thought that Jesus was against lawyers who interpreted the Scriptures, as a class, any more than he was against the Law itself. On the contrary, the pious interpreter of the Law was his ready-made friend. Such a one was very close to all the ideals Jesus stood for.

Once he said that the whole body of laws in the Bible, those that we know as the ten commandments and all the lesser ones about worship and human life and property, could be summed up in two: love of God and neighbor.

At this a lawyer praised him for having got the meaning of the Scriptures straight. Jesus saw that the man had spoken wisely and he said to him, "You are not far from the kingdom of God." (Mark 12:34) The reason why Saint Joseph and our Lady and Saint John the Baptist were such *just* persons —another word for holy—is that they let the Law of God, given by Moses, make saints of them.

The story is told of a French actress—alas, the poor French actress, basically a sodality type—that her sole comment on the ten commandments was: "Il y en a de trop"—"There are too many of them."

Don't laugh too soon. There's a little streak of that mentality in all of us. The speed limits are set too low, we think. The parking meters don't give you enough time for your nickel. The feud with a friend—heh! friend—seems the only reasonable way to keep in touch with a stinker or a catty type like that. The once-married man has all the charm. The nicest girl at work has a husband she ought to get rid of.

The list could go on all night. It would name all the cutting of corners we'd like to do to suit ourselves when it comes to laws and commandments. There's one big difference between a human law and a command of God, however, and we need to get it straight.

Laws are passed by governments—federal, state and local—to make it easier to be a good citizen. It is possible to argue them: "Our taxes are too high in this town."—"Why don't they put drinking drivers in jail instead of just revoking their licenses?" But in the main, good laws are made by good lawmakers. Keeping them is surely a key to considerable happiness as a member of the human family.

When God draws up his commands he doesn't need to consult a heavenly rule book on how to make life hard for his creatures. He looks in the human heart, and he makes his laws accordingly. That is why Christianity is such a simple religion. It is not something that can be captured in lists of ten or six or even 2,414. It is simplicity itself, as it came from the lips of the Master: "Thou shalt love."

We hope that by this time in your reading of these pages you're dipping deeper and deeper into the gospels and the Acts of the Apostles. The right way to follow up on the present chapter is to dig into Saint Matthew's gospel hard. Matthew is called "a Christian rabbi." His great concern is to show how Jesus is the new Moses, seated not on Sinai but on the mount from which he teaches. (See chapters 5, 6, 7).

"Of old it was said to you," says Jesus . . . "but I say . . ." He doesn't deny or twist the former meaning. He tells what Moses meant, at its highest and deepest.

God isn't out to make us miserable with rules. He sent his Son to set us free not from rules but from the bondage of rules. The great law of love of God and fellowman sets us gloriously free. Everything that holy Church requires us to do is just a way to make sure we'll enjoy our liberty best.

– 12 –

THE IRONY OF JESUS

There probably has never been a time in our national history when there was more attempt at comedy, and less genuine humor, than nowadays. Millions of dollars are being spent for well worked up "routines" and gags. What do we get for it? (Besides ulcers for last season's comic, when the Trendex ratings can't buy him a thirteen-week contract).

We get twenty million Americans, sitting stony-faced as they listen to something genuinely funny, and howling with laughter a few minutes later at the crudest kind of exchange of insults.

This pattern is having a real and a serious effect on our national character. We are becoming a nation of loud-mouthed bullies. The worst of it is, we confuse this diseased condition of soul with *fun!*

One autumn day last year, two Los Angeles teenagers drove up behind a man of eighty-seven and a woman of seventy who were proceeding at four miles per hour in a three-wheeled electric cart. The kids were in a 1951 sedan. You've guessed it! They pushed them off the road from behind—just for kicks.

"It's not against the law to push a cart, is it?" one of them asked. "The old people weren't hurt, were they?"

As a matter of fact, the man and woman had broken a few bones and suffered numerous cuts; but to be "hurt," in the language of these baboons, you need to have a fractured skull. A police captain in Los Angeles said afterwards, "We're up against a complete disregard for everything. You can't give a reason for it. The standards seem to have disappeared, and we have kids without standards."

What we do have are kids with a warped sense of what's

funny who have been helped to become that way by a billion-dollar industry. Not all comedy is cruel. Some of it—a fairly small percentage, it would seem—is good humored and uproariously funny.

Many Jewish people are in the field of comedy for a livelihood. Some of them are not especially amusing. They trade in jokes—buy them and memorize them and spiel them off—as they might trade in dry goods or real estate.

However, some of our most genuinely funny Americans are Jewish. Their gifts have enriched the national life greatly. One thinks immediately of Jack Benny, Sid Caesar or Danny Kaye. One of the funniest of American writers—you don't see him much, but you do see other people spouting his stuff—is a man named Goodman Ace. Look for his name some time on the television credits. When it says "additional dialogue by . . ." that usually includes anything really comical that was said by the funny man himself.

One important thing about Jewish humor is that it is always a little sad. Even at its highest peak it is touched by pathos. The reason is fairly easy to see. The Jewish character has been molded by suffering.

For centuries upon centuries, the Jew has felt the flick of the whip: Assyrian, Egyptian, Roman; then Polish, Russian, German. Persecution is like hanging. You never quite get used to it. But you do develop a few little ways to survive, and one of them is laughter. Often it's deadpan laughter, the kind you manage when your throat has just been cut.

Another mark of Jewish humor is that it makes its cleverest thrusts by saying the most outrageous things with a straight face, when the exact opposite is meant. There is a place in Herman Wouk's novel, *Marjorie Morningstar* (born "Morgenstern") where Marjorie, who has been loafing around the house for months, starts taking a shorthand course so she can get a job with a theatrical producer. Her mother has every good reason to suspect this burst of energy, and she says to her: "Shorthand! My God, watch out, you might end up useful."

We call that kind of speech "irony." It isn't exactly sarcasm. Sarcasm is usually out to hurt: to wound and leave a scar. Irony is different in that it includes a built-in antiseptic. It provides the opportunity for a person to look within and laugh at himself, which is nature's best remedy. Marjorie's mother was dead serious. If the girl had any sense at all she could see that her mother wanted to see her "end up useful" more than anything else in the world. *Irony is the last-resort language of an injured love.*

There have been oceans of ink spilled over the question: Did Jesus ever laugh? You can't prove from the gospels that he did or didn't. Of course the gospels are incomplete records. The men who wrote them had a very serious purpose: to print a word picture of the Savior of the world. Maybe they just left out all of his lighter touches.

One thing that is perfectly clear from the gospels is that Jesus and his friends lived a life of joy. Now, some joyous people are completely serious at all times. They may not be humorous, but they are always in good humor.

Jesus was the "man of sorrows" of the great poem in the Book of Isaia. (52:13 to 53:12) It is very clear that he was convinced of this. (Look up Mark 8:31; 9:30, 10:32ff.; Luke 24:25ff.).

Christ never made himself out to be a victim of fate, or a man so taken up with his own sorrows that he couldn't feel for another's. Yet, he *is* pretty serious in the gospels. No matter how you view him, our Lord can't be described as a comical sort.

Several traits about him are worth remarking:

–he never ridiculed or made fun of anyone except men of obvious bad will, genuine hypocrites. When he called Herod a fox, he wasn't tearing him down, just looking into his heart.

–he always dealt with ordinary people so decently that they came to trust him completely.

–he seemed so bent on the work he came to do that you feel he hadn't time for small talk.

Yet, he did exhibit a wry sort of humor from time to time. For example, when the man in the parable of the great supper gave as his excuse:

"I have married a wife and therefore I cannot come." (Luke 14:20)

"It is easier for a camel to pass through a needle's eye, than for a man to enter the kingdom of God when he is rich." (Luke 18:25)

"The scribes swallow up the property of widows under cover of their long prayers." (Luke 20:47)

That is pretty subtle, as humor goes. It wouldn't make you throw your head back and roar, but you might say to yourself inwardly: "Clever! What a grasp of the situation he has!" Our Lord wields a scalpel when he speaks, not a length of lead pipe.

Jesus is at his best—in that he is most a son of his people—when he says, along with the prophet Isaia: "The heart of this people has grown dull. Their ears have grown hard of hearing. They keep their eyes shut so that they will never see with those eyes—or hear with their ears or understand with their heart and turn back to me. Then I would have to heal them." (Matthew 13:15)

In other words, the Jewish mother's words, "Watch out, you might end up useful!" have the same flavor as Christ's caution to Israel: "Careful, Israel. You might end up sorry for your sins. Then I'd have to take you back, and I'm not sure I have time for that!"

This same Jesus, when he was too heartsick and tired for irony, said to his people, "Jerusalem, Jerusalem, murderer of the prophets . . . how often have I been ready to gather your children together, the way a hen gathers her chickens under her wings; but you would have none of it." (Matthew 23:37)

Irony, we repeat, is the last-ditch language of rejected love.

"When he threw that ax at me I thought I'd split."

Are you the funny man in your crowd, the poor man's Jerry Lewis?

The question is, even though you always leave 'em laughing, are your gags as much fun for the people they are *on* as the people they are *for?* Here's the acid test: *how much acid?*

There is a huge difference between the wit of Jesus Christ and the laughter of the devils in hell. When he gives a swift answer, he does it to make the hearer think. Jesus wants him to reflect, to become more of a person than before. When Satan plays the comedian, he wants to destroy a person utterly—strip him down to nothingness and howl after him with the hollow laughter that rings in hell. Sara in the Old Testament laughed at the promise she would be a mother, laughed it to scorn. The boy Chanaan laughed at his father Noah's nakedness. The passers-by laughed at the man on the cross. That is all so different from what Dante calls "the eternal light which loves and laughs."

"How can I describe this generation? They are like children sitting in the market-place and shouting at each other: 'We piped for you and you would not dance [Jesus, who went to parties]. We wept and wailed and you would not mourn.'" [John the Baptist, who went to none] Matthew 11:16ff.

What is your idea of fun?

When you joke, which are you more like—healer or heel?

-13-

JESUS, THE BREAD OF LIFE

God sent his Son to earth to show us the way to heaven. It's as simple as that.

Heaven is not some far-off place that happens to you when you die if you stay out of the messier kinds of mischief. It is by no means as simple as that.

Last summer Mr. Khrushchev, full of good lemon juice and bad catechism, said this to a United States correspondent:

"As to paradise, we have heard a lot about it from the priests. So we decided to find out about it for ourselves. First we sent up Gagarin, but he found nothing in outer space. It's pitch dark up there, he said; no Garden of Eden, nothing like heaven. So we decided to send another. We sent Titov and told him to fly for a whole day. After all, Gagarin was only up there an hour and a half. He might have missed paradise. Well, he came back and confirmed Gagarin's conclusion. He reported there was nothing out there."

Little Nikita was probably taught the difference between heaven and helium as a small boy. He just seems to have forgotten. If that's the kind of moonshine the priests were peddling in the Ukraine sixty years ago (and we doubt it), Marxism begins to look good.

For ourselves, we rather think that Khrushchev *minor* missed lots of C.C.D. classes.

God's Son came to earth because man had lost the way to heaven. Jesus said: "I am the way . . . he who follows me walks not in darkness but has the light of life." (John 8:12) The man who follows Jesus does not inhabit a murky outer space, but has the light of life.

God is light, he is all light. In the Gloria of the Mass we

call Jesus "Light of Light" because his whole being, as true God, comes from God the Father. Our Lord has another, further glory: not what he had with the Father from the beginning, but what God gave him to crown his manhood when he had finished the work he came to do. In explaining how he got this glory, Saint Paul says: "That is why God has raised him to such a height, given him that name which is above every other name . . . He dwells in the glory of God the Father." (Read Philippians 2:6–11).

Jesus sits at the Father's right hand, enthroned as Lord and Christ. This is heaven, the place where the glory dwells. Is it a "place"? It scarcely matters. We have to use words.

"Up" is scarcely a direction here. It means "where God is." The important thing is, *the glory of God is already shared.* It is meant to be shared further still: with you, and me, and every man who comes into the world. We are called to life, the same life Jesus Christ lives in the body *now.*

You might say that this is the whole of Christianity: a call to share in the glory Christ has at this very moment.

Christianity is not simply "being good." Many people who are not Christians are good. They keep the commandments, even though they may never have heard of them as such. They may not recognize the commandments as given to *them,* but they do live by them.

No, Christianity is not so much "being good" as it is "being different," totally different. It means being "graced," changed in body and soul, in thoughts and speech and ambitions. Nothing is quite the same again in our games, or work, or marriage, or citizenship—because Christ has come and we have received him. He leaves no one the same. Rather, he hopes to leave no one the same. His great prayer to his Father is that no one will remain alone, but that all may become one in him. (See John 17:20–21).

Now this is something unheard of and new in the world's history.

How does Christ bring about accomplishing the change? We scarcely need to review this, it should be so well known to all. First of all, he leaves to the Holy Spirit the actual work of changing. The Spirit is the sanctifier, the changer-into-Christ. This change comes about as a result of *a personal relation with Jesus Christ now, in his glory.*

Nobody can live through this contact with the Holy Spirit unaltered. Either he becomes a saint or he condemns himself.

When we say "this contact makes a saint of him," those are not just empty words. They have a meaning. They describe *the living contact between a person in this life and the person of Jesus Christ in glory.* Today—not centuries ago, on dusty roads in Galilee.

As of this morning there is no Jesus of the dusty roads—nor of the cross nor of the resurrection. But this morning there is a Lord Jesus *existing in glory.* He is not a soul or a spirit. He is a man like us who has a body and soul. His body is different from ours in that *it is deathless now.* Disease and pain cannot destroy it; food and drink no longer nourish it. It is completely changed. It exists *in glory.* More accurately, Christ himself exists in glory, and not just his body. He is the eternal Word, and he is glorified, perfect man.

The big question is, what is this glory we have been speaking about? Unless we know, we can't say, "I'm for that." Without understanding, we can only guess what the glory of Christ means. No one really has a passion to stand like a light and *shine* for all eternity. Glistening and gleaming is all right for a sunbeam but if you're a lively human being it has limited appeal—especially forever!

Of course anyone who thinks of Christ's glory in terms like that is running several catechism lessons behind Khrushchev. Christ *in glory* means Christ *fulfilled.* All that man could ever hope to be, *he* has become. The desires, the dreams of poor, striving mankind, Jesus realizes in himself.

Most important, in glory he has the power to be present to each one of us. In glory, he holds out to us the same sort of fulfillment that he has. That is the gift of glory: reaching our full perfection as sons of the Father.

If you and I are in Wyandotte, Michigan, we may dream of life in Ouray, Colorado, but our immediate influence in Ouray is pretty slim. To be "in the body" is to suffer this limitation of not being able to get around. But to be Jesus Christ in glory is to be in contact—direct, full and instantaneous contact—with this man in Wyandotte, that woman in Ouray, and millions of others all over the world.

What is Jesus' formula for remaining close to all those legions of human beings who have heard of him and believe in him? Is it that, being the Son of God, he can think himself anywhere he wishes? That's no answer. You and I can do almost as much.

Look at the title of this chapter. The answer lies there, of course. The bread of life is God's gift of the eucharist to us. *It is that sign by which the glorified body of Christ becomes present to us. If we eat of this bread, the glory that is his in the body is "sown" in us.* Like makes like, says the proverb. Saint Paul calls us "one body in Christ" because all of us who eat the sacrament-body of Jesus are being prepared to have a glorious body like his.

The eucharist, in other words, is *the great point of contact between Christ and us.* When we eat this supper of the Lord, we are getting ready to sit down at the heavenly feast. "Here I am, standing at the door and knocking," says Jesus. "If anyone listens to my call and opens the door, I will come in to him and have supper with him and he with me." (Apocalypse 3:20)

That is a description of every Mass, because in it we offer and receive the richest food that God has given to men: the body and blood of his Son. It prepares us for that great and unending meal of the Father's house, the heavenly eucharist, the blessing-in-praise that has no end.

"I am the bread of life," Jesus said. "Your fathers ate the manna in the desert and they died. The bread which I speak of, which comes down from heaven, is such that no one who eats of it will ever die. I am the living bread which has come down from heaven . . . He who eats this bread will live forever." (John 6:48–51, 58)

Hasn't the Master a forceful way of saying things? Yet, here is a puzzle. The same Jesus who said that eating his body and drinking his blood would bring life and not death, himself *died.* "Every time you eat this bread and drink the chalice of the Lord, you proclaim the Lord's death until he comes," was the way Saint Paul explained this to the Christians at Corinth. (I Corinthians 11:26)

Do we keep remembering the death, then, of one who conquered death? That's precisely the point. "Christ has been truly raised to life. He is the first fruits of those that have fallen asleep in death. For since man is the cause of death, a man also is the cause of resurrection from the dead." (I Corinthians 15:20–21)

Now we have all the pieces we need in this mystery—not *puzzle,* but *mystery*—of the life-giving food that is the Lord's body. First, we eat the food which is both a sign, and actually *is,* the body of the risen Jesus. It is the human body of one who has overcome death: he dies no more. It gives the possibility of deathlessness to those who eat it. It is like a seed which causes a tree, but at this moment cannot be recognized as a tree.

Second, it is a food which all of us who believe in Jesus Christ eat in common. It has the same effects on all of us, individually (an increase in the ability to love, a capacity for glory), and as a people of God. We are one Church, one body of Christ, because his one body is our common food.

Lastly, and most important of all, this food of the eucharist gradually fulfills us—makes us to be complete individuals who find happiness in union with others: Jesus the Lord and a whole host of brothers. The hardest cross in life, the deepest cause of unhappiness, is unfulfillment or a sense of incompleteness. You must experience it.

Are you taking the proper remedy for it—regularly?

–14–

JESUS, THE GOOD SHEPHERD

Thus Jesus spoke to them in symbol; but they could not grasp his meaning. So he went on:*

I AM the door of the sheepfold.
Those who climb in elsewhere
are robbers and plunderers:
to them the sheep will not listen.

I AM the door.
He who enters in through me
will be safe and sound:
he can come and go as he will, freely,
and will find pasture for his sheep.
The robber comes only to steal,
to kill, to destroy;
I am come that the sheep may
have life, rich and full
and abounding.

I AM the good shepherd.
The good shepherd
lays down his life for his sheep.
The hired man,
who works for a wage
but is no true shepherd,
has no real care for the sheep
since they are not his own;

* John 10:6–16, Tr. by Gerald Vann, O.P. *The Eagle's Word*, Harcourt, Brace and World, 1961.

so when he sees the wolf coming,
he abandons the sheep and runs
off, and the wolf harries
the sheep and scatters them.

I AM the good shepherd.
I know my sheep, lovingly,
each of them by name,
and they know me,
just as the Father knows me
and I know the Father
And I lay down my life
for my sheep.
Other sheep I have,
not of this fold:
I must lead them to pasture, too,
(and they will listen to my
voice):
so there will be but one flock
and one shepherd.

In the last chapter we were talking about the nourishment we get when Jesus is our food. The idea comes from him, of course, not from us. He keeps saying the same simple truths in a hundred different ways—always hoping that he'll get through to us. This time he talks about sheep and shepherds.

Now the chief task a shepherd has is to see that his sheep get good nourishment, and are safe. As animals go, sheep are a little dumb: timid, eyes down to the earth while they nibble away, ready to follow the crowd in any direction in case of panic. The threat of wolves or mountain lions causes the worst panic. But starvation and thirst are other possibilities if they aren't led to good grazing lands and water holes.

In a word, sheep remind us of us human beings generally. Men like to think they are independent, tough-minded, and all that. Actually, most people are fairly timid. They stay busy all through life holding down jobs, paying for a home, bringing up their children. They nibble away, eyes down, and are pretty frightened when great threats come along, such as war, or lesser troubles, such as losing their jobs. There are many other fears that grip people: for example, the thought that their children won't turn out right (fall prey to "wild beasts," one way or another); or will marry unhappily; or won't remember them when they, the parents, grow older (the constant fear of not having good streams and hillsides).

It would be a mistake to think that the hearers of Jesus didn't grasp his meaning in John's tenth chapter because they didn't know about sheep and shepherds. They knew *all* about them. Maybe some of you readers live on sheep ranches or near them. Most of you, though, have to rely on books or on a movie to know how sheep behave.

Not so the people of Galilee or Judea! They recognized immediately how a well-fitted sheepgate, usually bolted and barred, but swinging freely when opened, could mean life and death to the animals. The gate (or "door") was the best assurance the sheep had against their enemies, whether men or beasts.

Israel knew grazing as a way of life better than she knew city-dwelling or farming. The very name "Hebrew" once meant *wanderer or nomad:* not the sandy-desert kind, but the fringes-of-civilization kind. The nomad has no house, no farm, no bulky store of possessions. Unless he is to steal from other men, he has to transport his source of livelihood with him wherever he goes.

Flocks and herds are the best way to do this. When you read about Israel's great ancestor, Abraham, you see that his wealth is measured in "flocks, herds . . . asses and camels." (Gen. 12:16) His son-in-law, Lot, was rich in the same way: "flocks, herds and tents." (Gen. 13:5)

Often neighbors in biblical times had arguments when there were more cattle, sheep and goats among them than there was land to support them. (Even Abraham and Lot, who really liked each other, had to separate because of this). And *nobody* liked a sheepman in those days, any more than today. Why? Well, chiefly because the sheep used up too much of the water that people needed. Also they nibbled so close to the ground that they first ruined the land for farming and then caused soil erosion in the heavy spring rains.

Most important of all, the sheepmen would get the best out of everyone's land and then move on. They packed up their sense of responsibility with their goatskin tents and traveled off to the next valley. For this, all the farmers and the town-dwellers despised them.

Yet this was Israel's earliest way of life, and so she looked upon her great God as a shepherd set over her. "The Lord is my shepherd," this people prayed, "I shall not want . . . You are at my side with your rod and your staff." (Ps. 22: 1, 4) And in another psalm she sang: "O Shepherd of Israel, hearken, O Guide of the flock of Joseph!" Their forefather, Joseph, had fed them during days of famine, from his position of influence in the Egyptian court. Now it is the Lord himself who is being called on to care for Joseph's offspring: "Rouse your power, and come to save us." (Ps. 79:2–3)

You can see now, can't you, why, when Jesus spoke, "they could not grasp his meaning"? It should be pretty clear. Using figures of speech such as "I am the door," didn't confuse the listeners in the least. They were used to speaking in symbol language all the time. The heart of Hebrew poetry is figurative speech of this very sort.

No, they were troubled by two things: Jesus' repeated use of the phrase I AM, which was identical with the way the Lord had described Himself to Moses at the bush, and our Lord's claim to be *the good shepherd* who *gives life.*

That was enough to give pause to any Jew of Palestine. It seemed clear that Jesus was identifying himself with the limitless God, who had made the heavens and the earth. If there was any truth in Jesus' words, it was frightening to the hearer; if there was none, it was not a good way for a pious Israelite to speak. What Jesus' words amounted to was: "In all the praise you give to Israel's Lord, you speak to me."

Something else was involved, "the other sheep not of this

fold." In Jerusalem, crowds didn't *want* to understand that one, because they knew all too clearly what was meant. It was a threat—not veiled, but clear—that this teacher would go to the Gentiles, there to preach one great kingdom of God made up of Jews and non-Jews alike.

"And they will listen to my voice." That phrase has a thousand overtones. It is exactly what the prophets had said of old. If God's own people, so dearly beloved—ached for, longed for by him—do not hearken to his voice, he knows to whom he can go.

Nowadays we take a battery of psychological or IQ tests to prove whether the wheels are turning upstairs—or whether there are any wheels to turn. In the old days it was simpler: they asked whether a person knew enough to come in out of the rain? Could he blow hot soup? tell a hawk from a handsaw?

The Bible has a wonderful test of good sense in the things that matter most. Isaia says, in the Lord's name:

> The ox knows its owner,
> And the ass its master's manger;
> But Israel does not know me,
> My people have not understood.
>
> Isaia 1:3

Even the poor dumb beasts are smarter than people who don't put all their trust in God.

What do you put your trust in? Doing things "the smart way"? Lots of horsepower under the hood, or cash in the bank? Whatever it is, it won't do if it isn't the Son of Man who is a good shepherd to his sheep. That's really what our holy religion is all about: not about requirements and things to learn, but a lover who cares for us when we haven't the sense to care for ourselves.

We're all a little bit like sheep, even the keenest of us. Yet thinking for ourselves is absolutely essential. Getting all the facts isn't easy, mind you—never was, never will be. Do you tend to think of Catholicity as a great joint venture with Christ the leader, who thinks along with us and sometimes for us?

That is what it is, of course. He knows all that can happen to us, good and bad. He will be door and shepherd and all to us, if we do but one thing. We have to unstop the ears of our pride and listen to his voice.

–15–

THE AUTHORITY OF JESUS

You've probably seen the television show "Youth Wants to Know." The kids who appear on it are quite brainy. They are representative, if not of all modern youth, at least of those most likely to "want to know."

Youth wants to know many things, but "Who's in charge here?" isn't one of them. Someone, however, is always in charge. That's authority. There's nothing wrong with this—but it can be aggravating, because it's a system that works all the time.

Psychologists say that human beings have all sorts of needs, wants and drives. It doesn't seem that the "will to be bossed" is one of them.

Is this the case? Is authority a "pain in the neck"? Before we give a snap answer, we need to consider three separate yet related terms. One is *anarchy*, another is *authority* and the third is *discipline*.

Anarchy is the state of things when there's no one in charge. That's exactly what the word means in Greek: "no boss." Mutiny at sea, rebellion on land, bedlam in the school bus: all have the one thing in common—total lack of authority. Nobody thinking, nobody calling the plays; everybody shouting. Are they happy? Yes, probably—the way small children and the insane are happy when they're let loose. There's a sick joke that has a mother saying to her children with a sweet smile: "Go out and play in traffic, dears." That's the spirit of anarchy: no bosses, no rules—and no protection. Why? Because no one *cares*.

Authority is a different matter. You know what it is without needing a definition: *Authority is the voice of someone who knows or who has the say in things.* When the people who have the say also happen to know, it makes things much easier. Serving under authority is hard for all of us. But when authority is both intelligent and kind, obeying it is less of a chore.

Discipline is perhaps the hardest of the three to define. It doesn't mean repression of liberties. It isn't a term for bossing a tough gang like the Capone mob, or having the strictest teacher of the school for homeroom. Discipline is the fine art of being able to learn—of being a disciple. The man who can be taught has disciplined himself. The loudmouthed idjit hasn't. Discipline is something that comes from inside a person, not from outside. Unfortunately when we speak of it we usually mean "enforced discipline," and that's the degradation of a very fine word.

From the gospels we learn that one thing that drew the crowds to Jesus was that *he spoke with authority*. More than that, *he acted with authority*. That doesn't mean that he bossed people around! That was the last thing the poor peasants of Palestine needed. The Romans told them what to do. Rich landowners told them what to do. The religious leaders told them what to do. All three classes spoke in firm, hard tones, demanding enforced discipline.

Consequently, any teacher who came along and said, "This is *really* it," wasn't going to attract a crowd very readily. But we miss the force of the gospel word "authority" entirely if we think that all it meant was a firm tone in Jesus' voice, a piercing eye, and a conviction that he was a true teacher sent from God.

No, "authority" was a word with a special religious connotation for the Jews. It didn't mean any *human* way of acting, but the power of *God himself*. That is exactly what the crowds thought they saw in Jesus of Nazareth—divine power. And oh, how they longed for it!

They had been without a true prophet for more than four hundred years, until the Baptist came along. They thought the heavens were closed against them. The Lord had visited his people in Moses' time, when he led them out of Egypt by his mighty outstretched arm. Centuries later he set them free from a second captivity, this time in Babylon. But that was now more than five hundred years ago. Persians, Greeks, Romans—everyone had trampled on them since. Had they any hope? What could be the meaning of God's promise made to Abraham, renewed in the Law given to Moses, repeated sternly but lovingly through the mouths of all the prophets? Oh, how they wished they knew!

Then there came this strange man from upcountry, Galilee, who had never been trained as a rabbi, but *who spoke and acted with the very tone of God.* That is what is meant by the *authority* of Jesus. *He was a man who acted with the full power of God.*

The word *authority* has *author* in it, and that word means someone who gives growth or increase. Not only the people who turn out three-hundred page books are authors, but all those who start something and see that it continues. President Kennedy is the author of the Peace Corps, a plan for aiding underdeveloped nations by helping them to help themselves. General George Marshall was the author of the Marshall Plan for feeding Europe after World War II.

But the great author of all that is is the God who is the Father of our Lord Jesus Christ. The most wonderful thing that he begins in us is our faith in him. This spirit of perfect confidence he means to bring to fulfillment in us. He would never get such a wonderful work started if he didn't intend to end it fully, in the glory of union with Himself.

Jesus' authority was not just meant for the Jews. He saw to it that it would reach all of us—through his Church. When someone says to you, "The Roman Catholic Church is a religion of authority," what does that mean to you? Do you automatically say to yourself: "It certainly is a religion of authority. Not only does it have a set of rules for what to do and what not to do, but it even has a whole hierarchy of people telling other people what to do." This sounds as though you are missing the whole point of the teaching of Jesus. If God is a God of *love,* he doesn't stand around barking orders all day. If Christianity is a religion of *love,* there must be more to it than rules and commands.

There is—a great deal more. Try to think of it this way. You have been given the Spirit of Christ in your hearts. That gives you the power to cry out to God, "Father!" as only a son can do. You are sons in the only Son. When your Father speaks to you through his Son, in the gospel proclaimed in the living Church, he does so with *authority.* What he is the author of is a whole way of life that is love.

We listen to him attentively, in the spirit of disciples. We are well-disciplined, in other words, so that we may learn. We love God's authority, and that of his Church, because it never means anything but good to us. It is a *voice of love,* and it demands an answer on our part *in terms of love.*

Right now you're a Catholic, a member of his Church. Do you think you will always be one? If Christ came back in glory, would he find faith on the earth?

Many people who were born Catholics aren't Catholics any more. They have thrown off the authority of Christ, or else they've said that his authority hasn't any connection with the Catholic Church. Do you know why they've done this? Generally, it's because they never understood what his authority meant. They thought it was a set of rules: rules about marriage, about birth control, about obeying the bishop. How little they knew about the inner nature of faith in Christ. It is true, Jesus said, "If you love me, keep my commandments," but the operative word in that sentence is love. If all Christianity consisted in was keeping rules, there'd be very good reason to drop out. The Pharisees had rules, plenty of them. That is why Jesus came to set men free. His whole task was to set men's feet on a path of love and obedience leading toward a kind Father. Does your Catholic faith mean *that* to you?

If it doesn't, you've got a worry on your hands because you're mixed up in something really big that you haven't got a grip on. Do you think that the Catholic religion is nothing more than a list of rules and regulations for people who can't think for themselves? You must begin to realize that you are committed to a religion that is a willing response of love to a love that surrounds you like the air you breathe. Start "breathing" this love—and you'll find a lifetime of happiness in store for you.

in [illegible] began to realize that you are enmeshed in a [illegible] that is a whirling vortex of love [illegible] that surrounds [illegible] the [illegible] "incredible" [illegible]—and you'll find a lifetime of happiness in store for you.

–16–

THE SINLESSNESS OF JESUS

If you have ever served Mass or taken part in a recited Mass you will remember having said in the Confiteor, "quia peccavi nimis," which means, "because I have sinned exceedingly . . ." Have you really sinned exceedingly in thought, word and deed? That's a question everyone must answer for himself. It's a question that has to be faced, because the great work of Jesus was to save us from our sins. If we don't understand something of sin, we will never understand him. The best description of Jesus Christ we can give is: "He is the one who is everything that sin is not."

One thing that is very clear from the gospels is Jesus' complete lack of sorrow or regret for his own actions. He associated with sinners, and they were strongly attracted to Him. But he never indicated that what he had in common with them was sin. He could forgive them—and he did—only because he himself was sinless.

In Chapter 5, when we were speaking of Jesus and the demons, we tried to point out the difference between what are sometimes called our sins and *sin;* between the human weaknesses that are part of everyday life, and that unspeakable revolt against a holy God which we call evil. It is, of course, the difference between venial sin and mortal sin, the latter being the tragedy of bringing death of spirit to ourselves.

To be death-dealing, sin needs to be something that is a seriously wrong, of its nature; but it must be more than that. It must be carefully and hatefully thought out. If it is a question of passion, it must be willingly allowed to grow. Then, and then only, does it qualify to keep us from possessing the holy God forever.

That information may come as a relief to some readers who

have gone through agonies of worry thinking that all "sins" are serious sins. Generally speaking, the more you worry the less likely they are to be mortal offenses against the love God has for us.

There are some Christians, however, who have another danger to contend with. That is the notion that practically nothing they do is seriously sinful. People with this outlook tend to think that sin is some kind of thing or stuff that you "catch," the way one has sinus trouble or scarlet fever. And just as most people think they're never going to die, or can't pick up a disease, so they have a tendency to think that no matter how they behave on dates, deal with their parents or their marriage partners, lie and cheat, they can never qualify as serious sinners.

But of course they can. That is the frightening mystery of freedom of choice. You *can* choose against the love of God that enfolds you, and you *can make it final.*

The thing to fear in life is gradually coming to lose the idea of the holiness of God. Venial sins, when they are multiplied, bring this about. Venial sins are small acts of unfaithfulness, of broken honor, of disloyalty to a lover who has a claim on our perfect loyalty. These little choices against a great love bring a person to a point where he doesn't care, one way or the other, any more.

Now a person who no longer cares, but who had a friend once whom he loved, can turn on that friend in hate. *He can hate no one else as he can hate someone he once loved.* This turning-in-hate we call sin, when the friend is God. "Sin" in this sense has no adjective to go with it. It needs none. It is just sin, simply sin—the mystery of a free human being turning on his loving Father in rebellion. We could call it "mortal," perhaps, but no qualifier is necessary to establish that it means an end to God's life in the soul.

We call Jesus of Nazareth sinless because rebellious thoughts such as these never had a moment's place in his mind. What the Father wanted, Jesus in his turn wanted and wanted with all his human strength. He desired it immediately and fully. This longing for God's will to be done, this adoration of his will once it is known, we call in a creature *holiness*. In God, his very will which is he himself, *is* holiness.

Jesus was holy in two ways, the way of God and the way of man.

You mustn't think of his human holiness as an endurance contest: Jesus constantly biting the bullet, bent on obeying the Father's will regardless of how painful he found it. It wasn't that way at all. He recognized God's will immediately. His human will fell right in with it, even though later this would cost him something in physical pain, or in his emotions, or wherever else men pay a price.

We must insist on this because some followers of Jesus have their major problem not with "sins" nor with *sin*, but with advancing in holiness. They get as far as knowing that this is mostly a change that the Holy Spirit brings about in them, not one that they work in themselves. At first they trust in his action as fully as they know they should.

Then they begin to wonder, "How long can I hold out? Do things get easier? Will I ever get to recognize God's will fairly readily? The way it is now, I go through torments of indecision, and when I act I am never quite sure if what I choose is the right thing to do."

The problem may be different in your life. It may take this form: "Knowing God's will is not so hard for me. It's *doing* it that causes the grief. Will I ever leap to do it, as Jesus did in his earthly life? I want to be a saint, but the very *attempt* is so great a hardship that it makes me want to chuck the whole business."

A furious crowd shouted at Jesus once, "We are the descendants of Abraham, we have never been slaves to any man. What do you mean by saying 'You shall be free?' "

"In very truth I say to you," said Jesus, "everyone who commits sin is a slave. The slave has no status in the household, but the son is at home there forever. If then the Son sets you free, you will be free indeed." (John 8:34–36)

What a sense of relief those words of Jesus bring! He gives

security—not gilt-edged, locked-in-the-vault security. Neither is it the rustproof, mothproof kind. He does provide relief from life's greatest captivity, fear. You are sons, he says, along with the only Son, because the Father has made you so. You have the run of the house—his house, my house. Be holy, as I am holy. If the Son sets you free, you will indeed be free.

The secret of Catholic life, Christian life, is that in it you throw off your fears. The big fear is that there is a hard set of laws to keep that you won't be able to keep. But this is getting things all in reverse. *Christian life is freedom from this fear and from every other fear; it is power to live as a family member lives.*

A son is perfectly at ease in his own house. He doesn't tiptoe around in the kitchen. This is his home! All his actions come naturally to him there, from turning on the TV to sitting down at table with the rest of the family. If it is a happy home, his actions are not only natural, but a pleasure to him. He knows exactly how to behave himself and he gets a certain delight out of behaving the way he does.

It wouldn't do to pretend that there's no challenge in Christian life. Being a red-blooded citizen of the United States or Canada these days, and staying faithful to God, can make a pretty stiff combination. The points worth stressing, however, are these:

1. growth in holiness is something God brings about in us more than we do ourselves (though we must accept freely his gift of holiness);
2. Jesus wants to share his own holiness with us;
3. gradually it *does* work out that way—in other words, each time we choose to make our will agree with God's will, the choice becomes easier. And, each time we do so we make the choice faster and with more happiness. Why? Because we come to resemble Christ. The family likeness between the only Son of the Father and his many sons, becomes evident to all; it even becomes plain to us.

Our Lord, when he was provoked at his enemies in Jerusalem, once said, "Which of you can prove me guilty of sin?"

(John 8:46) He wasn't just hurt or insulted by them, as you or I would be. No, Jesus knew he was being accused of selling out to his Father's great enemy, Satan. Jesus, who was *total holiness,* was being called *unholy.* That was the one thing his honor and his love for his Father could not stand.

You've got a perfect right—yes, *you*—to holler "foul" when anyone links your name with serious sin. Serious sin is not a necessary part of life. Christ is acting through his sacraments all the time to destroy the possibility of sin in us. The chief "effect of sin"—of Adam's sin—is the individual mortal offense against God's love; but *by God's grace it need never take place*. St. John goes as far as to say: "We know that no child of God commits sin." (I John 5:18)

We repeat: *a serious fall doesn't ever need to happen,* no, not once in life. You can go from early childhood through to the grave as someone perfectly charitable, perfectly chaste, perfectly honest and perfectly truthful.

Did you know you could? Had anyone told you that the sinlessness of Jesus is something that you can possess if you let the Holy Spirit have his way in you. Read the whole first epistle of St. John, which makes this very explicit.

Your cue is there.

Why don't you take at face value the Christian teaching on the total victory Jesus can win over sin *in you.*

– 17 –

THE PRAYERFULNESS OF JESUS

"Beads and prayerbooks are the toys of age," wrote the cynical poet Alexander Pope. Everyone knows what he is referring to: the special religious fervor of those advanced in years.

Maybe he's right. Many elderly people attend weekday Mass. ("Cramming for their finals," one wiseacre has put it.) Afternoons and evenings, too, one often sees older people in the subdued light of the church. Their movements are stiff and slow; they're in no hurry now. They have no obligations. No one waits for them. With gnarled fists, they clutch their rosaries or leaf through their missals.

The bitter poet seems to have accused these senior citizens falsely. How could he have known that they had been prayerful most of their busy lives; that they'd never had enough leisure to pray as much as they wanted to. Now, with time to spare, they are making up—and they care little what others may think. There is no embarrassment about them. They kneel or stand as they please, following the Way of the Cross at the pace that best suits them. They love God much and they speak to him freely. They have known pain at his hands, but they have also known great joy. They pour out their hearts to tell him so.

How wonderful it is, though, when the young are prayerful. They are not "benched" by arthritis or age. They have perfect freedom of movement. There are a thousand interesting things they could be doing. Yet, they choose to pray . . . to pray much!

Praying, however, isn't the same as *saying prayers.* Not at all. Sometimes, in fact, *saying prayers* just gets in the way of real praying.

What, then, is prayer? Prayer is an experience of closeness to that Holy One who is our God. At times we will be moved to speak to him with words. This is not always the case, however. It is enough that we have a sense of his presence, that we are aware he is near, that we know our lives are touched at all points by him who alone is sacred.

He *is*, and we *are not*. He is the All-Holy; we are but dust and ashes. We bow our heads at the thought of him. We are ashamed. We shrink before the mystery of his great majesty. Our own nothingness humiliates us. Yet, there is a bridge by means of which we may reach him. That bridge is his Son. Jesus is God and man. Therefore, we and God have Jesus in common. Moreover, the love that the God-Man bears us casts out any fear we might have. *Awe* and *dread* before the almighty God remain, but *fear* is no more! The blood of the cross is a tide that has washed all fear away.

Occasionally you meet a young man or woman who gives much time to prayer. It may be a college football player who is in the chapel whenever he isn't out on the field or at the books. Or, perhaps it's a young mother who comes to the church at 1:45, though she doesn't have to pick up her first-grader until 3:00. When these people pray, they don't *say* much. They simply experience the majesty of God, and words become unnecessary—sometimes impossible. They just kneel or sit there and "drink him in."

The prayer of Jesus was prayer such as that. He could kneel in perfect silence for hours, drinking in the glory of God. God was the very condition of his being, so to say. As the sun is to plants, or temperature is to bodily health, so the great God and Father was to Jesus of Nazareth.

It would be wrong to give the impression that prayers made up of words or actions are not important. Our *greatest Christian prayer* is an action (more properly an act) of Christ: the Mass. Here his work of saving us is done in the sign language of bread and wine, of gestures and of prayers. And in the very heart of the Mass we find the prayer that he himself taught us, the Lord's prayer. It has always had a place of honor in the Mass, to prepare our hearts for the body of the Lord.

The Church has many prayers with words—our Mass book is filled with them. They are simple and direct prayers which speak all the thoughts and desires of men.

Indeed, the gospels give us ample evidence that Christ prayed with words. He prayed for his friends: "O Father! I will that those whom you have entrusted to me shall be at my side where I am. I want them to behold my glory, the glory you bestowed on me because you loved me before the world was founded." (John 17:24)

He prayed for his enemies: "Father, forgive them; they do not know what they are doing." (Luke 23:34)

Jesus prayed the night of his arrest, while his whole being shuddered in dread at this evil which was taking place: "My Father, if it is possible let this cup (i.e. this bitter dose of pain) be spared me! And yet, not as I will but as you will." (Matthew 26:39)

Most of all, however, he prayed during his lifetime in joy and praise to his heavenly Father. "He looked up to heaven and after uttering a blessing in thanks broke the loaves into portions." (Mark 6:41) "Father, I bless you thankfully for giving ear to me . . . I know that you will always hear me." (John 11:41ff.) "I praise you with a blessing, Father, Lord of heaven and earth, for hiding these things from wise and learned men and revealing them to simple ones." (Matthew 11:25) Here Jesus referred to God's great work. Through the life and death of Christ, God worked out his plan to save men, a plan which, until that time, was hidden in the depths of his being. In his prayers, Jesus acknowledges that marvel.

This acknowledgment of man's salvation is the core of the whole business. If you think that prayer means "delight in saying prayers," you're quite wrong. Nor does it describe a feeling of inner satisfaction that God is there as a partner in conversation. Actually, you may have no awareness of him in the sense of being joined to a conversation partner, and yet engage in some fine prayer.

But of course you must have *some* awareness of him, for as we have said this is the meaning of prayer. To be present before God, in some way, with any part of your mind or heart, and to wish to acknowledge the marvel of his goodness in saving us—*that* is prayer.

If you get discouraged, therefore, about trying to pray, it may be that you are on the wrong trail. Take, for example, this business of *feeling* that your prayers are being heard. Whatever God is like, the one thing about him we can be sure of is that *he is completely different from us.*

It's true, we describe him in words very similar to the words we use for people: spirit, person, father, goodness. But these words all add up to a description of human beings. They can never capture the reality which is God. This is something no human tongue can describe.

That is why people who tell you that they have nice, cozy conversations with God (who answers them, moreover!) probably have a very limited idea of God. They're really talking to themselves.

This problem of prayer to the divine majesty would be reason for real discouragement if it were not for one thing. That thing is the *prayer of Jesus.* You see, there is a close union between what is man and what is God in Jesus. His manhood unites him with us, making him our brother. Because he is also God, however, Jesus is much better able than we are to think human thoughts of what God is like.

We find prayer hard. Jesus finds it easy. It is his element, just as water is the element of a fish. He thrives on prayer. It is conversation with *men* that is strange to him, for men are not holy as his Father is holy.

Yet, he longs to talk to men so that he can put them in touch with his Father. When we want to speak to God, therefore, we should do it through Jesus. He is man as we are men. We can picture him in our imaginations, read his very words in the gospel. He comes *alive* to us. He leads us to that God whom we could never come to know on our own.

When we pray to God through Christ, the words we choose are not our own. They are supplied by the Holy Spirit, whom Jesus sent us for this very purpose. The Son *leads* us in prayer, but the Holy Spirit *provides the power* to pray. "He will guide you into all the truth," our Lord said, just before he left us. The one great truth we need guidance in is how to speak words of trust and love to our Father who is so high above us. On our own, we might make a botch of the job. Jesus, therefore, leads the whole Church in a chorus of praise. To be of the Church is to pray gloriously under the skilled direction of Jesus Christ our head.

The correct term for the Church's prayer under the headship of Christ is *Liturgy,* that is, a work of the people of God.

– 18 –

JOY IN FOLLOWING JESUS

A Mr. Joyboy is one of the main characters in Evelyn Waugh's novel, *The Loved One,* in which he pokes fun at American burial customs. Mr. Joyboy is the chief mortician at "Whispering Glades," and he has charge of the Slumber Room, the Orchid Room and all the other plush accommodations for "viewing." He takes extreme pleasure in his work, deriving great satisfaction from making a big fuss over preparing the corpses (whoops! "loved ones").

Every crowd has its joyboys; anything for a gag. They don't get enjoyment from fussing over the dead. They're all wrapped up in *life.* Everything is a big joke. A laugh a minute.

Joy can mean lots of things. For instance, it is a girl's name. *Joy* is supposed to make dishwashing a . . . pleasure. *Joie de vivre* is "zest for life" in French, with all sorts of overtones of wacky gaiety. *Filles de joie*—they're not such happy types at all, but in a grim and gritty business.

There was a time when "Joy to the World" meant that Christ the Savior had come—now it means four weeks of unbearable TV assault on the ears.

What is the definition of true joy? *Joy is what comes to him who heeds the commands of Christ and dwells in his love.* "I have spoken thus to you, so that my joy may be in you," Jesus said, "and your joy may be complete." (John 15:11)

That definition of joy isn't at all like the other examples. If it is the correct meaning of joy, then serious people who seldom smile can be filled with joy, and those with the noisiest laughs may never know it. In such case, sorrow is not necessarily the opposite of joy, for the keeper of Christ's commands may lose mother or husband in death, may be bitterly disappointed in love, may never succeed materially in his life's work, and yet continue on in the love of God without interruption. *All through his time of trial and sorrow, he never loses joy.*

A joyful person doesn't mean a fixed grin suspended in midair like the Cheshire cat's. He needn't like early rising, algebra, or broccoli, homely girls or overtime at no extra pay. If he delights in *doing God's will in a spirit of love,* however, he will know joy.

Contrariwise, some of the youthful joyboys of our time who get a thrill from cruising around town in a car with a case of beer don't know much joy. They are sad cases and sad soaks, in the strict sense. Nothing has ever given them deep-down satisfaction. Their young lives are terribly unfulfilled.

Depression and gloom are their companions—daily, not just "the morning after." They know little of the joy of Christ, and so in the deepest sense they do not know joy.

The idea of joy has a long history among the people of God. If you examine the Old Testament carefully, you'll see that religion is always a *sacred* and a *serious* business for Israel, but it is never a *glum* business. Long-faced religion—the Puritanical type—is simply unheard of there.

One thing you do find in the early days of Israel is a wild, frenzied sort of dancing and song—religious "exaltation," it is called. It is much like the revival meetings you read about at which people get "carried away in the Spirit." All this happened back in the early biblical period when the religious practices of Israel were quite different from what they came to be later.

The notion of joy is the thread we are following, though. Like cheerfulness, it keeps breaking in. For the Israelites, joy was all tied up with music and song. It was the state of heart of anyone who gave praise to the Lord. The Lord, in turn, rejoiced over the love his people bore him, just as a newly married man rejoices in his bride. (See Isaia 62:5). The people bowed their knees to God in adoration and sang the joyous songs of David and the court musician, Asaph.

After their bitter exile in Babylon, they came back singing. When they set up the worship of the Lord in the temple, again they did it with joyous song. "They sacrificed great sacrifices that day . . . God had made them joyful . . . and the joy of Jerusalem was heard afar off." (II Ezra or Nehemia 12:42)

The meaning of all this can't be missed. What the Bible is saying is that music, song, religion, and joy are all mixed in together. You can't have one of them, in the truest sense, without the others. Does this make sense to you? It should, because aside from the fact that it's as clear as crystal in God's holy Book, it seems to be written everywhere in the book of the human heart.

Yet, it would be foolish for us to suppose we could experience real joy in the Lord by merely delighting in music and song. A lot of impressive singing and organ music (if your parish is fortunate enough to have these) is meaningless without everyone's joining in much of the time. In turn, the popular participation which the Church is stressing in our day can be empty formalism without that necessary consent of each one to follow Christ in one's heart.

In other words, *religion is not chiefly an experience of emotion.* But, conversely, *there is no true religion without emotion.* Whoever seeks the joy Christ promised, and does so without joyous celebration in song, has exchanged Christianity for some other religion.

For a while—perhaps for a century or more—a persecuted people can hold on to its Catholic faith without the religious ceremonies, without its song. After that (and usually well before it) *joy in believing* steadily dies among this people, almost by a law of nature—a law of grace, we should say. Unless whole congregations can full-throatedly sing out their

Kyrie and their *Sanctus,* their *Hospody Pomilui* and their hymns full of great music and great words about the mystery of faith, they will gradually lose first their enthusiasm and later their balanced Christian faith.

See if this isn't true with you. When was the last time you were carried away with joy at the experience of having brothers in Christ? Was it, for example, at Sunday Mass in your parish church when the *entire* congregation prayed and sang together? Or was it, perhaps, in the municipal auditorium last October, or a city park a year ago, when you and your fellow Christians, in full-throated chorus, sang together the praise of God through Christ the high priest. Whenever it happened last, we'll wager it was too long ago.

You may have wished to experience this spirit of joyfulness more often, but you have not had the opportunity. You discover that this Christian joy business is not so easy, when so few in the Church seem committed to working at it. How about happiness through silence—can this be more readily experienced? Think it over carefully. Is it not true that happiness and peace are hard to come by unless we regularly experience Christian exultation and joy?

"Then I heard a voice like that of a great crowd, like the noise of rushing water and of mighty thunders, and it cried, 'Alleluia! Now the Lord our God Almighty reigns! Exult and shout for joy and give him glory, for the marriage of the Lamb has come.'" (Apocalypse 19:6ff.)

This is a word picture given us by one of the inspired writers of the early Church. It explains the kind of joy there will be in the last age of the world, the time we are in now. It refers to Jesus Christ, the Lamb of God, and his love for a holy people—a people as close to him as a woman is to a man in marriage. Christ spoke of how his friends should share in his joy, when he prayed, "I speak these words so that they may have my joy within them in full measure." (John 17:13) "Be always joyful," says Saint Paul. (I Thessalonians 5:16) "Count it all joy . . . when you meet . . . trials." (James

1:2) "All joy is yours . . . The Lord is near." (Philippians 4:4–5)

We want him near. We need that joy. In the eucharistic celebration he comes nearest of all. Then, let's sing out the praises of the Lamb as if to burst our throats.

JESUS AND HIS OWN PEOPLE

Whether you happen to come from the State of New Mexico or the Province of Ontario, chances are you have a lively attachment to your home place. If you go off to the armed services, to college, or traveling where your work takes you, no one will mind it too much if you push the glories of your native state or province. People will rather expect it, in fact.

It's the same thing with being an American, a Canadian or a Puerto Rican. There are few men so attached to the whole human family in general that they can't work up a little special enthusiasm for people of their own country or nationality. We praise this outlook. We call it the virtue of *patriotism* or love for one's homeland.

When these natural sympathies get out of hand, however, a diseased state of mind sets in. This is termed *nationalism* or, sometimes, *racism*. Premier Mussolini of Italy and Germany's *Führer*, Adolf Hitler, in recent history, were *nationalists*. Both were trying to restore to their people a pride in their achievements as a nation, but they went too far. They carried their nationalism so far, in fact, that the rest of the world was forced to defend itself against these two dictators, even to the point of war.

Perhaps you've heard something about Hitler's racist theories. He believed that the branch of the Aryan peoples known as *Nordics* was the "master race" (in German, the *Herrenvolk*). As a scientific theory it isn't worth much, but if you happened to be tall, blond and handsome and lived in Germany thirty years ago, it could be very appealing. Hitler himself didn't fit his own description of a Nordic, but it could have cost you your life to say so in public.

Jesus of Nazareth was born into a people which held some

views much like the ones just described. In the case of the Israelites, however, the situation is rather complicated. You see, the undeniable fact was that God had done special favors for the people Israel. Israel was his son, his beloved. Israel was his chosen people. The entire Old Testament is a record of God's agreement (covenant) with this priestly nation, an agreement to make it great above all the peoples of the earth. This was an agreement which he swore he would never go back on. (Read Genesis 17:4–8; 28:13–15; Exodus 6:7; Leviticus 26:45; Deuteronomy 7:7–11; 30:15–20).

But, this did not mean that the Lord God wasn't interested in the other peoples on the globe. In the first book of the Bible (Genesis chapter 10), you find a list of tribes from all parts of the Near East. Israel was only one out of this group, and the Israelites knew it. They were certain that *God was Lord of the whole world,* even though he did have a special interest in them. After all, they said in their holy books that man, not just Israelite man, was made in God's image and likeness. (Genesis 1:26ff.)

When those religious reformers whom we call the *prophets* came along, part of their message was to remind the people that the Lord willed to save *all men* and not only them. Many people didn't like to hear this, for they had become very *nationalistic.*

By Jesus' day, the idea of the unity of the human race and the importance of every individual was losing ground even among the rabbis. After they returned from the Babylonian exile in 538 B.C. their nationalism reached such a fever pitch that some were teaching that only a circumcised Jew could know happiness in "Abraham's bosom," an expression they used for a blessed after-life.

You pick up a hint of that in Saint John's gospel, where he says very briefly: "Now Jews do not associate with Samaritans." (John 4:9) The point of Saint John's story was precisely that Jesus, although a Jew, did not consider himself too good to associate with Samaritans. He did that very thing, as a matter of fact, when he spoke with the Samaritan woman at the well of Israel's great forefather, Jacob. Our Lord had made a friend from among these people who were traditionally the enemies of the people Israel.

At every chance he got, Jesus scolded his own Jewish people. ("This wicked generation" was his favorite description of them!) On many occasions, he compared the heathen nations favorably with his fellow Jews. He spoke of the Queen of Sheba (Matthew 12:41ff.), the widow in Sidon back in the days of the prophet Elia, and the general in the Syrian army, Naaman (Luke 4:24–27), in more favorable terms than he did the Jews.

Jesus seemed to take special delight in multiplying examples of good religious conduct among foreigners, and of his own people's ingratitude to God. "Nowhere in Israel have I found such faith," he said once, after a Roman soldier expressed certainty that Jesus would cure his servant. (Matthew 8:10) *Nowhere* in Israel, mind you. Though Israel was still the favored son—the people God meant to have for his own—Jesus found more faith in a Gentile. On one occasion a crowd of his own people were quoted by Jesus as saying to him: "We sat at table with you and you taught in our streets."

What will his reply be when it comes time to judge them? "I do not know where you come from. Out of my sight, all of you." (Luke 13:26ff.)

Instances could be multiplied of the anger Jesus showed at the sins of his own people, the annoyance he exhibited toward their pettiness. Yet he loved them deeply. It would remind you of the way parents put their children in their place when they get fresh. Whammo! They lose their tempers and sail right in because they love them so much. Mothers are forever praising the local talent: "Why can't you be more like Imogene McNasty? You never see *her* doing a thing like that!" Yet, these are the reproaches that are born of love.

The thing to look for in the gospels is not the flare-ups of Jesus, but his overall approach to "the Jewish question." Read carefully and you'll see that, in a word, he was mad for Israel. He had to be; after all, didn't he do always the things that pleased his Father? And wasn't the Lord God partner to a romance with Israel that went all the way back to Moses' time in the Sinai desert? "I passed you by and saw that you were now old enough for love . . . I swore an oath to you and entered into a covenant with you; you became mine, says the Lord God." (Ezechiel 16:8) Here, the prophet was referring to God's special love for Israel. The love that Jesus bore it could never be less than that.

And what a marvelous love he had for the holy city! He wept at its faithlessness: "O Jerusalem, Jerusalem, the city that murders the prophets and stones the messengers sent to her! How often have I longed to gather your children as a hen gathers her brood under her wings, but you would have none of it." (Matthew 23:37)

Jesus' extreme concern for Israel is evident in his policy on preaching and teaching. "I was not sent except to the lost sheep of the house of Israel," he said. (Matthew 15:24) In other words, the gathering of the scattered flock, which had been the work of all the prophets, was equally his task. When Jesus first sent his twelve friends out to preach his instructions were, "Do not go in the direction of the Gentiles, nor enter the towns of the Samaritans; but go rather to the lost sheep of the house of Israel." (Matthew 10:5–6)

Does that sound strange to you? You knew Christianity was a world-wide religion, of course, and have always heard that Jesus came to save *all* men. Well, he did, but his first and biggest concern was "his own sheep." (John 10:3)

We can understand why Israel will always be the favored offspring from the parable of the prodigal son. Upon the wasteful boy's return home, there is great celebration. The father says to the older son, who is angry and refuses to join in the festivities, "My son, you are always with me, and everything I have is yours. We *had* to celebrate this happy day, for your brother has returned." (Luke 15:31–32) The people Israel is the elder brother. Everything God has belongs to him. Israel's position was never safer. Yet, when the Gentiles came to believe in the true God, after centuries of false religion and sinful conduct, it was necessary to rejoice. The Jewish people were asked to join in, in celebrating the wanderer's return.

We have it from the lips of Jesus himself that, "Salvation comes from the Jews." (John 4:22)

Eileen Duggan, an Australian poet, wrote a piece some years ago called "Nationality." Toward the middle of the poem, these lines occur:

> Discountried and diskinged
> And watched from pole to pole,
> A Jew at heart remains a Jew—
> His nation is his soul.

It has to be that way, don't you see? The promise made by God was to his own, special people—forever. Though the land God gave the Israelites for their own was taken from them by the Greeks and the Romans, God never changed his promise.

Some of the Jewish people have a homeland once again, the state of Israel. Praise God for that! But they are not there on the same terms as we find in the biblical promise.

Nevertheless, God is found faithful to his promise even apart from that holy land. Because he isn't tied down to one little portion of earth, we must look to see what relation he continues to have with his chosen people if we are to discover whether he is faithful or not. God passes the test. He proves his faithfulness by the love he bears his beloved Son Jesus, the perfection of the chosen people. Though Jesus became "a light of revelation to the Gentiles" (Luke 2:32), he never stops being "a glory to the people Israel." God is in a continuing relation of love to all Jews, forever, because of his promise, and its wonderful fulfillment in becoming incarnate in Jewish flesh and blood.

But, are we not all sons of the one Father? And is not Jesus himself our peace? "Gentiles and Jews, he has made the two one, and in his own body of flesh and blood, has broken down the enmity which stood as a dividing wall between them." (Ephesians 2:14ff.)

However, *the Jewish people will forever be the first heir to God's promise.* We must never forget that. God "has them with him always." All that he has is theirs. For he has never said, "I gave my promise to Israel once, but when I sent my Son I called the whole thing off." That would be nonsense. God cannot act in such a way. He is the Lord, and he changes not.

We who are Gentiles must hold our elder brother Israel in awe—this rightful son of the household. If we do not, we make a mockery of an ever-faithful God. Read chapter 9 of Saint Paul's letter to the Romans. Then read chapter 11. Then adore the inscrutable will of God for the mysterious love for his people Israel that will forever be his.

Saint Paul wrote: "By their (Israel's) false step, salvation has come to the Gentiles." (Romans 11:11) In other words, God permitted Israel's defection in order that all men might have an opportunity for salvation. If the Jews had accepted Jesus immediately, Christianity could scarcely have become universal. Undoubtedly, they would have kept this faith as narrowly national as they had kept Judaism.

Is their rejection final? Paul, who continued to love his people despite the folly of some, and who proudly wrote of himself, "I also am an Israelite, of the posterity of Abraham, of the tribe of Benjamin," made it very clear that *their rejection is not final.* He wrote, "A partial blindness only has befallen Israel, until the full number of the Gentiles should enter." (Romans 11:25) After the nations have had their full opportunity to enter the Church, Israel will have its second chance and not fail. Why? "Because," said Saint Paul, "God does not revoke his gifts and his call." (v. 29) God loved his son Israel in ancient times, even when he was faithless. He loves him still. He always will. He shall yet bring him home to himself, the loving Father!

—20—

JESUS, THE SUFFERING SERVANT OF THE LORD

Some families still have servants. Not many, but some. Nowadays, most people who have someone working for them have an employee rather than a servant. You see the difference, don't you? *Servant* is a word that is passing out of use in this part of the world, because the social order it describes is disappearing. A more correct way of expressing it would be to say that, generally in the Western world, the relation of master and servant is giving way to that of boss and worker or employer and employee.

It is no disgrace to be a servant or, in modern terms, an employee. The only time this arrangement becomes disgraceful is when one man treats another *as his servant*. To order a person around and to forget his dignity completely is the greatest injustice one human being can do to another. It doesn't matter whether this involves an army general and a private or a corporation's president and vice-president. No one is ever free to disregard the basic worth of another individual.

Many times the "servant" may really be the master. For example, the filling-station employee who gives you a bright smile and says, "At your service!" is far from being at the bottom of the social ladder. By his courtesy and willingness to help, he qualifies as master of the situation. On the other hand, a man who seems to be the master, if he is governed by pride and the desire to domineer those who are close to him, is actually the slave.

This should all be very clear to you. It is well to recall it, though, because the notion of "servant" (which was close to that of "slave" in ancient times) plays a big part in the gospels. We cannot understand Jesus Christ in glory, King and Lord over angels and men, unless we know that in the days of his flesh, one of the proudest titles he claimed was servant.

His mother, too, was a servant. You remember how she agreed to God's plan as soon as the Angel Gabriel had explained it to her. "Regard me as the humble *servant* of the Lord," were her words. "May all that you have said be fulfilled in me." (Luke 1:38) And when she praised God's goodness in song for choosing her to have a part in man's salvation, she called herself "his lowly maid." (Luke 1:48)

In this, both she and her Son were like their people, "his servant Israel," whom God had kept faith with ever since Abraham's day. (Luke 1:54) Although the people Israel were servants, they were not "slaves to any man," as the crowd angrily told Jesus once during an argument (John 8:33); they were trusted servants of a loving Master. "You whom I have called my servant, whom I have chosen and will not cast off—fear not, I am with you; be not dismayed; I am your God." (Isaia 41:9ff.)

When their prophet Isaia wrote that way, putting speech on the lips of the Lord himself, Israel did not feel humiliated at being called a servant. This was a high title. So much confidence had been placed in them as the Lord's servant that the word conveyed to them only the holiness and splendor of their Ruler in heaven. "I will strengthen you and help you, and uphold you with my right hand of justice" (Isaia 41:10), he promised this servant of his.

There are many other Bible passages where "servant" is a term of highest praise for the people of God. Often, too, it will stand for a pious individual Israelite, such as the author of one of the psalms, or the inspired writer of the Book of Wisdom: "Give me wisdom, the attendant at your throne, and reject me not from among your children; for I am your *servant*, the son of your handmaid." (Wisdom 9:4–5) When God gave this gift of wisdom to the servant who asked for it, he became a magistrate, a king, or a temple builder

—all of which roles were fulfilled holily in the Lord's service.

The relation between the Lord and his servant, the people Israel, is a tender one of love and affection. "Servant" in the Bible means trusted son rather than laborer or slave. How could anyone hope for a stronger bond between God and a holy nation than is expressed in the following lines:

> "Remember this, O Jacob,
> you, O Israel who are my servant!
> I formed you to be a servant to me;
> O Israel, by me you shall never be forgotten:
> I have brushed away your offenses
> like a cloud, your sins like a mist;
> return to me, for I have redeemed you."
>
> (Isaia 44:21ff.)

Since serving the Lord had placed Israel at the very top among the nations, it is no wonder Jesus taught that "he who would be a prince among you must be your servant, and he who would be a leader . . . must be your slave." (Matthew 21:26ff.) He wasn't the type to hand out empty advice, either. He practiced what he preached. Because he was a true son of Israel, he, too, was a servant. Remember his words: "Why even the Son of Man did not come into the world to be served but *to serve* and to give His life as a ransom for many." (Mark 10:45)

The statement that he gave "his life as a ransom for many" is the clue to the whole idea of service as the Scriptures use it. You don't just *serve* the Lord. You pay the price for the honor of being his servant. This price is the offering of your life—your *total* being—to God.

It may seem harsh to put it as directly as that, but there's no other way to express the great truth that Jesus taught. He was a good and faithful Servant and entered into the joy of the Lord, but not before he had paid the price of his own life.

To understand why it had to be so, we need to know four wonderful songs or poems in the Old Testament. These are called the Servant Songs. They all come from the same prophet's pen, that inspired author who wrote the second part of the Book of Isaia. The theme of the four poems is the same: that the Lord has a servant who will suffer much at the hands of Israel's enemies. The sufferings of this servant will end in death, but this will be no tragedy, for his guilty brothers will be judged innocent as a result of the death of this innocent sufferer. (Read these songs in Isaia 42:1–8; 49:1–6; 50:4–9; 52:13–53:12).

The Servant Songs are sad, all right. Reading them reminds us of the sufferings of Christ as the gospel describes them:

> He was pierced for our offenses,
> crushed for our sins
> Upon him was the chastisement that
> makes us whole,
> by his stripes we were healed.
> We had all gone astray like sheep,
> each following his own way;
> But the Lord laid on him
> the guilt of us all.
>
> (Isaia 53:5–6)

The interesting thing about these beautiful prophecies is that, in our Lord's day, their real meaning was lost. The students of the Scriptures read them in such a way that they made the prophecies refer to the sufferings of the Lord's enemies! But the clearest thing about the Servant Songs is that the servant is God's great friend, not his, nor Israel's, enemy. In a general sense, this servant is the people Israel who must suffer for being faithful to the Lord. Upon more careful examination, you will see that a specific individual is being spoken of—a single member of this holy, suffering people.

> If he gives his life as an offering for sin,
> he shall see his descendants enjoy a long life.
> (Isaia 53:10)

What Jesus, the Messia, did was to take these sad poems that seemed to describe defeat, and attach them to the figure of the glorious leader whom the people were waiting for. None of the rabbis of his time wished to do this. Nevertheless, Jesus said that Israel's Messia and the Suffering Servant were one and the same person. He said, more shocking still, that *he* was that person. "The Son of Man will be betrayed into the hands of men and . . . put to death . . . They will mock him and scourge him and spit upon him . . . (he will) suffer much, be rejected by the elders, the high priests, and the Scribes, be put to death, and after three days rise again." (Mark 9:31; 10:34; 8:31)

To make sure that His followers had understood him in his lifetime, Jesus said during his risen life: "This is the gist of the Scriptures: the Messia must suffer and on the third day rise from the dead." (Luke 24:46) He described it as necessary for the Messia to suffer so that He could enter into his glory.

It is easy to say that everyone baptized into Christ must suffer and die with him if he hopes to enter into his glory. It is difficult, though, to understand exactly what this will mean to *you*. Until he sends you suffering, almost nobody in the world can get across to you what to expect.

Don't worry about it now; but when the blows begin to fall, or the taunting begins, or the attacks from without and within threaten, think of your model, Jesus, the suffering servant, and say to yourself: "Well, here we are! Right on schedule. The servant is no better than his master. My master is the Lord of all because he served his brothers in suffering. Why can't I give it a try?"

point greater of a single member on this [illegible] concerning people.

> [illegible] his life as a ransom for [illegible]
> A myriad [illegible] descend [illegible] along life's [illegible]
> [illegible]

Thus Jesus, the Messiah, did [illegible] It seemed to describe defeat, and struck terror to the heart of the glorious leader whom the people were waiting for. [illegible] the tidings of his [illegible] that [illegible] Messiah and the suffering servant were one and the same. [illegible] that for you [illegible] the Son of Man will be betrayed into the hands of men and [illegible] certain death [illegible] will mock him, scourge him, and spit upon him [illegible] He will suffer much, rejected by the elders, the high priests, and the scribes. He will be put to death, and after three days rise again. (Mark [illegible])

[illegible] that the followers had [illegible] the time Jesus and [illegible] Thus is the [illegible] Son [illegible] the Messiah must suffer and on the third day rise from the dead. [illegible] death [illegible] For the Messiah suffers so that [illegible] enter into His glory.

It is good to know that each one baptized into Christ and [illegible] together with Him [illegible] to understand [illegible] Christ [illegible] suffering [illegible]

The [illegible] that when the storms [illegible] of the [illegible] think [illegible] the suffering servant [illegible] Christian [illegible] better [illegible] the Lord of all because He saved His brothers [illegible] Why can't [illegible]?

-21-

ARE YOU HE WHO IS TO COME OR LOOK WE FOR ANOTHER?

The poet Belloc has a verse that runs,

> *Kings live in Palaces, and Pigs in sties,*
> *And youth in Expectation. Youth is wise.*

The name of that piece of solemn nonsense is "Habitations." "Home is where the heart is," says the proverb. We dwell in what we wish for, in other words. So it isn't such a nonsense verse after all. The dwelling place of youth *is* expectation.

Now *expectation* and *hope* are first cousins. In one sense there isn't too much difference between them. Perhaps *expectation* has a ring of "I-think-it-will-happen" about it; *hope* has more the idea of "I-want-it-to-happen-but-don't-know-how-it-will-come-about." If that distinction is a correct one, then *hope* is the weaker word.

Yet, when *hope* is used in a Hebrew or a Christian sense, it has always been, and still is, a strong word. It describes a state of mind that is rooted in the known reality of God's love. He wills only good for us. The knowledge that we have of his will and his plan for us fills us with holy hope.

He will do everything, in other words, that is necessary to help us be with him in his glory. The utter certainty that this is so, we call HOPE.

That seems to put things off quite a bit, doesn't it? No matter what age you are you tend to think that you won't be with him in his glory for a good number of years. Must we say, then, that hope has to do with a distant day in that it looks ahead twenty or fifty years? That would make a kind of useless virtue out of it—one that is almost bound to dry up for lack of exercise.

But of course that would be to think of hope much too narrowly. Hope is something that is ever-present, since God's care and his plan to save us are ever-present. Confidence, or trust based on certainty, is a thing of every moment. So hope is as actual to us now as our needs are. We hope at all times because our progress toward the Father, in Christ, continues at all times. The continued need of God's help, plus the continued certainty of receiving it, add up to a hope which is always active.

In Jesus' day, the people of Galilee (his home territory in northern Palestine) and Judea (the south, where Jerusalem was located) were full of expectation. It would be good to report that they were also full of hope. But since *hope* is the stronger, truer, religious word, it is impossible to make such a report. In those times, great crowds of people had a trust in God's power to save them that was like a counterfeit bill: the eyes weren't quite straight, the lines were wobbly. They trusted more in their being sons of Abraham than they did in Abraham's God. The majority of the Israelites were more interested in being free politically than in being free from the slavery of sin.

We shouldn't, of course, neglect mentioning that there were many who had a solid hope that the Lord would be faithful to his promises. Among these were Mary, the mother of Jesus: "He has given help to Israel, his servant," she sang, "mindful of his mercy to Abraham and his children's children, forever" (Luke 1:54); old Zachary, father of John the Baptist: "He promised by the lips of his holy prophets that he would save us from our enemies and from the hands of all who hate us" (Luke 1:70–71); and Simeon: "Now Your promise is fulfilled; for my eyes have seen the deliverance which You have prepared before the face of all the nations." (Luke 2:29–31) These three saints under the Old Law represent a large class known as the "pious poor" in Israel—those whom Jesus praised in his first two beatitudes. (Matthew 5:3–4)

These are three cases in which those who possessed hope

in the Lord, in its truest sense, lived to see their hope fulfilled.

All through the gospels we pick up hints of a popular belief in a mysterious personage referred to as "He who is to come." You get a reference to it in the question which the disciples of John the Baptist put to Jesus, having been sent by John for this purpose: "Are you he who is to come, or shall we look for another?" (Matthew 11:3) Jesus answered by naming some of his miracles which were roughly the same as those listed in the book of the prophet Isaia. (26:19; 35:5f.) These miracles were given by Isaia as necessary signs of the "last days": the blind see, the deaf hear, the lame walk. Jesus reported these things and the greatest marvel of all: "The poor have the good tidings proclaimed to them." (Matthew 11:5)

Jesus used the same words about "the expected one" to describe himself when he quoted a psalm that says, "Blessed is he who comes in the name of the Lord" (Matthew 23:39); and after feeding the five thousand with five loaves and two fishes, the people marvel and say, "This is indeed the prophet who is to come into the world." (John 6:14; see Deuteronomy 18:15)

The people of our Lord's day had all sorts of titles for the person God would send to deliver them. They also had a variety of notions about what "deliverance" or "salvation" meant. As we've hinted above, the really good people knew that being set free from the weight of sin was the big thing. Still, all of them—even Mary and Zachary and Simeon—quoted passages out of the Scriptures that spoke of their deliverer as scoring a smashing victory over Israel's enemies, who were also supposedly God's enemies.

At times, "the expected one" is called "the Holy One of God," whether by a demon (Mark 1:24), or by the fisherman friend of Jesus, Simon Peter. (John 6:69) The angels at Bethlehem call him a "Savior" (Luke 2:11); so do the Samaritans, those neighboring people sandwiched between Galilee and Judea who had the same beliefs as the Jews, by and large. (John 4:42)

It is to a Samaritan woman at Jacob's well that Jesus says, when she tells how she expects "the Messia who will tell us everything," "I am he who am speaking to you now." (John 4:26) That was a remarkable thing to say to a foreigner! He almost never told a fellow Jew he was the Messia. No doubt this was because the word *Messia* had come to mean all sorts of wrong things in his day.

Messia is the Hebrew word for an anointed servant of God. In Greek, the way to say it is *Christos*. It is a title, therefore, not a proper name. "Jesus is the Christ," we who believe in him say, as we might say, "John F. Kennedy is the president," or "Elizabeth is England's queen."

The word *Messia* was on everyone's lips during Jesus' lifetime. That, in a way, was what was wrong with it. Jesus warned his friends, "If anyone says to you, 'Look, here is the Christ; see, there he is,' do not believe it." (Matthew 24:23) So there must have been plenty of candidates for this honor in his day.

"Can it be that the rulers have really come to know that this is the Christ?" the crowds in Jerusalem asked about Jesus. "Yet . . . when the Christ comes, no one will know where he is from," some objected. (John 7:26ff.) Evidently there was some mystery associated with his appearance on the earth. More than that, on the basis of their own Scriptures the devout had come to believe that the Christ would continue forever. (John 12:34)

Great was the faith of the common people in the coming Messia, and they asked, seeing Jesus "When the Christ comes will He work more signs than this man works?" (John 7:31) Obviously, Jesus was doing as many and as great wonders as these men of good will were ready for in their wildest dreams. Yet not all of his miracles together satisfied the Scribes and Pharisees, who kept asking for a "sign" in proof of his claims. (Matthew 12:38)

Let us put the pieces in this puzzle together now, to discover just what Israel hoped for in the Messia. First, the Jewish crowds thought their God would do great things for them, and they were right. He had promised it. They thought that when he sent his anointed king to save them it would be the last age of the earth, and in this they were right, too. They likewise thought that Israel would defeat all her enemies in battle, and that the Messia would rule under God over all the peoples of the earth.

Here they were very wrong. You might say that Jesus was put to death because he told them how wrong they were.

For what our Lord did was change the popular idea about a lightninglike "coming of the kingdom." He let them know that the Messia and the Suffering Servant were one and the same, *and he was that one.* The people were terribly slow to get the idea; some of them never got it. Even after he rose from the dead, his best friends asked an old, old question that was by then clearly the wrong question: "Lord, will you restore the rule to Israel at this time?" (Acts 1:6) He tells them that they'll never know God's secret answer to that one, so will they please get on with spreading the news of salvation to the ends of the earth. *And, this advice to get busy with the spread of the kingdom is just what you and I need.*

When Jesus came, he was the Messia of Israel's hope. In the hearts of believers, those with true hope, his coming was glorious, triumphant, although many others did not see this.

When he returns, when he comes back to us, his glory will be made plain to all, believer and unbeliever alike. Meanwhile it is hidden. Like God's love in the soul, it can only be seen by the eye of faith.

Let us sum up in black and white what we Christians hold about the Lord's Anointed who has come in human flesh:

Jesus Christ, our hope of glory. The Son of Man who will come back to us on the clouds of heaven. The Lord, the just judge, who will say, "Come, you blessed of my Father."

All this we can be certain of. This is the substance of our hope.

–22–

THE RAISING OF LAZARUS

Can you remember clearly your first personal experience of death? High school is the time when many have their first taste of "fell sergeant death," so swift in his arrest. Seeing a member of one's own family, or a school friend, lying still in a satin-lined casket can be a bitter experience for youth. Do you recall your first encounter with this intruder?

It seemed so unfair at the time. No one had ever warned you that death could be so cold, so motionless, so final as this. When the dead person's body went into the earth—if he was the first person close to you to die—life seemed strange and unreal for days!

When someone alive and active yesterday lies dead today you wonder how people can go about their business, especially if that person was very close to you. You are puzzled that some who suffer a loss can be so calm about sending telegrams to all the relatives and calling on the phone to make the "arrangements."

An empty feeling, hard to describe, comes over the young person who experiences his first death. That emptiness is real, palpable. It crowds out completely what seemed impossible to displace—life! Everything appears somewhat false and useless for weeks after death—if it's a boy or girl's first death.

As people grow older they get used to death—death *for others*. That's the deceptive thing about it; when you think about death or talk about it it's always someone else's. Paradoxically, the less you think about death, the more easily you grow accustomed to it.

Victory over death was accomplished in the life of Jesus of Nazareth. It is his great achievement. When Peter delivered the first Christian sermon, he said that the Master had not been left in the grave; his flesh did not see decay. "God has raised up this Jesus—of that fact we are all witnesses." (Acts 2:32) Though Jesus has a tomb, his is very different from all other tombs. It is empty. He sits at the right hand of God. The proof that God had made Jesus Lord and Christ, said Peter, was that no tomb could hold him. His proper element was not death, but life.

Are you familiar with the mention of Lazarus in the song sung at a funeral, as the body is carried down the aisle of the church to the door? It is called *In Paradisum.* The words go like this:

> *May the angels lead you into*
> *paradise,*
> *The martyrs receive you at your*
> *coming*
> *And guide you into Jerusalem the*
> *holy city.*
> *May the angel choirs bid you*
> *welcome—*
> *Give you rest eternal in the company*
> *of Lazarus,*
> *Once a wretched beggar.*

This was the Lazarus of Christ's parable. (Luke 16:19–31)

There is another Lazarus in the gospels. You will remember that he is the man whom Jesus brought back to life after he had been dead four days and his body had begun to stink with decay. The true story of this Lazarus has an important message in connection with your death, and with Christ's death. Let us examine it.

Jesus had been a good friend of a certain two sisters and their brother, whom he used to visit at their home in Bethany.

Lazarus lay dying, and his two sisters sent word of this to Jesus. The Lord did not run off in haste to visit him, however, least of all to cure him on the spot. He very calmly said when he got the news: "This illness will not result in death. No, it is to promote the glory of God. Through it, the Son of God is to be glorified." (John 11:4) Then for two days Jesus didn't make a move. Rather strange conduct, wouldn't you say?

Jesus then went back to Judea (where both Bethany and Jerusalem were located). He knew that his enemies were out to destroy him; he also knew that he would accomplish the work he came to do in the time the Father had given him, neither more nor less.

First, Jesus told his friends that Lazarus was asleep, meaning to say in hidden language that he was dead. They missed his point, so he came out with the direct statement: "Lazarus is dead. For your sakes I am glad I was not there, so that you may believe. Come now, let us go to him." (John 11:15)

Do you see how Jesus thinks? It is always in terms of the unveiling of the mystery of God. This unveiling God accomplishes slowly, through His Son. Jesus came for the very purpose of helping make this *revelation* (unveiling). He does not wish to uncover completely the mystery of God's love for us —that would be impossible—but to share it, to enlighten us on the unspeakable riches of his tender care.

The funeral had already taken place when Jesus arrived at the outskirts of the town. Martha ran to tell him the sorrowful news. Jesus and Martha had a profound conversation right there on the spot. It is given in the gospel of the Mass on the Day of Death or Burial. (See John 11:21–27). Jesus promised Martha that her brother would live. She was a pious Jew, and had the same convictions about the raising up of the dead from their graves as Jesus did. She already believed in what Jesus reminded her of and said so. It is as if a priest were to comfort someone at a funeral, and the person were to agree with what was said because he had the same faith as the priest. Jesus and Martha held to the belief of the Pharisee party that the dead would rise again.

Then Jesus said to her: "I am the resurrection and the life. He who believes in me will live, even if he dies; no one that lives and believes in me shall be dead forever. Do you believe this?" "Yes, Lord," she replied, "I firmly believe that you are the Messia, the Son of God who was to come into the world." (John 11:25-27) Do you see the point? She goes from a general faith in the resurrection to a particular faith in Jesus as the Christ.

Once Martha had said that, Jesus had accomplished all that he had hoped for in Lazarus' death—with her at least. Then he went off to the rock-hewn tomb of Lazarus to try to move other hearts to have faith in him, and in the Father who had sent him. Making his way through the noisy, wailing crowds, he disregarded the stench of a body four days dead, went into the little cave and cried out strongly, "Lazarus, come forth." (John 11:43) When Lazarus emerged, bound hand and foot with linen in the custom of those times, Jesus said, "Unwrap him and let him go."

Many believed in Jesus that day. Some did not. Those who did not reported to his enemies this latest sign of power, and the supreme council in Jerusalem (the Sanhedrin) began to plot against his life.

That's the way it is with the Son of Man. You're either with him or against him. There is no middle road. The more power he shows from on high, the more you trust him, or hate him.

If you believe in him, you do not fear death—your own or anyone else's. You know that it is chiefly a way God has to show forth his glory—the glory of the resurrection that he will share with men who have the faith in Christ that Martha had.

–23–

THE MEALS JESUS TOOK

Jesus did nothing without a reason. The more you read the gospel, the more you see the truth of this statement. He never acted on the spur of the moment, nor gave answers thoughtlessly. At the same time, there is no evidence that Jesus lived under any strain. He moved from one action to the next with a calm certainty which said, "I do always what pleases the Father who sent me."

(Read John 8:27–30 for Jesus' policy on the conduct of his life; also John 4:34, where he considers doing the Father's will his meat and drink).

This attitude of deliberateness is seen in the least of his actions—even in the meals he took. There is no record of his taking meals in the normal routine fashion. It is true, he was hungry after his long fast in the desert, as anyone would be. (Matthew 4:2) Later, when vast crowds pressed around him, in his adopted town of Capharnaum, he and his disciples "could not even take a meal." (Mark 3:20) Yet the impression is clearly given by the gospel that every time he ate or drank, he did so to promote the kingdom of God.

This can be seen in his visits at the homes of "sinners." In the gospel this word does not usually mean evil men. Like a modern definition from Moscow, it meant what the religious leaders decided it should mean, namely people who did not keep the Law of Moses as those in power interpreted it. That is why when we read that Jesus "reclined at table (stretched out to eat a banquet meal, a Greek custom) with sinners," we know that the company wasn't half bad. (See Mark 2:15–17).

Eating with tax collectors was another thing our Lord did fairly often. That was a slightly different matter. Tax collectors were almost certainly crooked, in an official sort of way.

When we read in the gospel, for example, about Zaccheus, "a high official among tax collectors and rich as well," (Luke 19:2), we know both what his bank balance was and how it got that way. Surely he was a dishonest man. Yet Jesus ate with Zaccheus because he was rich and therefore greatly in need.

Jesus said, "Zaccheus . . . today I must be your guest."

Down Zaccheus scrambled from the tree he had climbed to get a better look at Jesus. He welcomed the famous teacher joyfully. Jesus said of him, presumably during the meal he took, "Today salvation has visited this household, because he, too, is a son of Abraham. After all, it is the mission of the Son of Man to seek and save what is lost." (Luke 19:9–10)

One thing we need to know about Jesus and meals, especially the formal meals he took as an invited guest, is that the Old Testament period looked upon the banquet meal as a sign of something holy. A father and his family would celebrate sacred meals at a common table laden with rich foods. An example of this is the great supper held at harvest time which is called *Sukkoth* (Feast of Booths, or Arbors). A rich man would also invite guests in great numbers when his son was being married, in those days. When he did this he was celebrating the marriage of the Lord to Israel, as well as that of his son to his bride.

Most sacred of all, however, was the banquet meal taken after a sacrifice had been offered. In this practice, whatever was offered to God—say a ram, a lamb, or some grain—was given by God back to the Israelite who offered it. It was "consecrated," changed into God-like food, by being offered to God. When God returned it to the people, they ate as their food something that properly was his. In doing so, they came very close to God. After all, they were being nourished by sacred food—food that had been made God's special possession.

Now Jesus was a faithful son of his people. He took part in

all of Israel's customs, the religious ones above all. He attended the usual banquets on the three great feasts of pilgrimage to Jerusalem each year (Passover, Weeks, and Booths). He also attended many a wedding banquet and family celebration.

The special celebration that the Jews of Jesus' time hoped for was the banquet of the End Time or the last age of the earth. They would eat it when the Messia came, they thought. It would be then that the close friendship with God that had dawned in the garden of Eden would be renewed.

In the meantime, every meal in celebration—the Passover and all the other feasts—provided a way to speed the coming of the Messia. This would bring God's deliverance. Under his anointed king, the holy people would sit down at God's table and eat and drink in his kingdom. The Jews were sure of this, just as sure as you are that the sun will come up tomorrow.

Jesus put a stop in his lifetime to a lot of foolish guessing about the future. But one idea that he never discouraged was that the last age would be like a great meal of celebration. "You have stood by me in my trials," he said to his friends toward the end of his lifetime. "Therefore, just as my Father has willed that I should inherit kingly power, so I in turn vest in you the rights of kingship; you shall eat and drink at my table in my kingdom . . ." (Luke 22:28–30)

Our Lord once told a parable about a great supper. In it, it was made very clear that the master's house had to be filled to capacity. (Luke 14:22) Even if the host needed to force the guests to come in, he meant to have a full house. Surely this was a reference to the way Jesus felt about his kingdom, the Church. It would be filled first with Jews, then with Gentiles; and there would always be room for more.

Jesus did say, however, that not everyone will sit at his Father's table. He put it this way: "Many will come from the east and west and in the company of Abraham, Isaac and Jacob, will recline at table in the kingdom of heaven." (Matthew 8:11) At the same time, born citizens of that realm will be thrust out into the night because they do not have the faith that a heathen Roman soldier had. They will complain, our Lord predicted; they will cry out bitterly: "We ate and drank under your eyes, and you taught in our streets." (Luke 13:26)

Jesus will say to such people: "I tell you, I do not know who you are. Get out of my sight, you pack of evildoers." (Luke 13:27)

Other people, who do have faith, will be able to say the same thing of Jesus as Saint Peter did: "We . . . ate and drank with him after he rose from dead." (Acts 10:41) This will be perfectly acceptable to the Father. In Peter's case, he is naming the special reason why he and the other disciples had been given the task of preaching the good news. They had already taken a meal with Jesus, Lord and Christ, in the kingdom of God.

This meal was the Last Supper, that final sacred meal that Jesus ate with his twelve friends. All the food and drink he ever took led up to this meal. When, on another occasion, he had multiplied the bread by miracle at the lakeshore, he acted just as his Father had done through Moses when he sent manna from the sky to feed the Israelites in the desert. Jesus' miracle recalled the miracle in the desert and it looked forward to the great banquet of the Last Supper.

The chief sign of discipleship that Jesus left behind him was given at the final meal eaten before the coming of God's kingdom in glory. Jesus said as much. In fact, he took a vow not to drink wine again until the kingdom of God was set up. (Luke 22:16) Days later, when it was established at a new level by his resurrection in glory, he was free to drink "the fruit of the vine" again.

Jesus is the *true* bread from heaven—we have his word on this—as opposed to the manna which was only a sign. He said that if men eat his body and blood they will have life to sustain them until the Last Day. He gave them his body and blood at the Last Supper. He gives this same body and blood to us, in the eucharistic celebration. (Read chapter 6 in St.

John's gospel; it is the closest John comes to discussing the institution of the eucharist).

Mealtime is happy time, charity and love time. Have you found it so? Would you be ready to have Jesus come to your dining room table, your plant or school cafeteria, and offer you his body and blood there? Do you treat your family meals as sacred banquets, serving God in all that you say and do while you're eating?

If your meals mean all this to you, each one of them is tied in with your next eucharist. Both your meals and your eucharists will then look forward to the table of the Lord at heaven's high feast.

-24-

JESUS ENTERS JERUSALEM

There is excitement in store for anyone who gets the chance to travel. One thrill that travel may bring you is the sight of the cathedral dedicated to our Lady in Chartres, France, as you approach it from Paris. The outline of the huge church pierces the skyline, rising from the flat meadows and farms like a ship sailing on a sea of wheat.

Another such thrill is the one that comes with first spying the cathedral at Pisa in Italy, with its famous leaning tower, as you approach it through the hill country from Florence.

Most people experience a clutching at their hearts when they see the Capitol at Washington. Or when leaving the United States aboard a ship, they watch the Statue of Liberty fade in the waters of New York harbor. Greater still is their elation when, on their return, the Great Lady, the symbol of freedom and security, welcomes them home.

People sometimes feel cheated because no one has ever told them how much it would move them to gaze suddenly upon these sights. All these buildings tell something about God, something about man.

Since our chief concern in these pages is Jesus of Nazareth, we will want to know what sights moved him most deeply. Great natural beauties? Man-made wonders?

Surely the most moving sight that Jesus ever gazed on was the holy city of Jerusalem. Its chief feature for him was the temple being built by Herod the Great. Psalm 121 sang (and Jesus must have prayed it often): "I rejoiced because they said to me, 'We will go up to the house of the Lord!' And now we have set foot within your gates."

Psalm 83 took up the same theme: "How lovely is your

dwelling place, O Lord of hosts! My soul yearns and pines for the courts of the Lord."

These snatches from the psalms underline the point we wish to make. There was no major distinction between sacred buildings and other buildings for Jesus and his people. Their whole outlook was sacred. The capital city, Jerusalem, was not just a fine city; it was the stronghold of their God. His shrine or sanctuary was the central place in it. A holier or more splendid setting anywhere in the world they could not imagine. Everything in Jerusalem shared, in some way, in the holiness of the central shrine.

Jesus loved Jerusalem because it was the city of King David, his ancestor of a thousand years before; but also, and above all, it was his Father's city. The temple was there with its holy of holies (that dark, empty chamber where only the high priest, a descendant of Aaron, went once each autumn to sprinkle blood for the people's sins). This room had long ago housed the stone tablets of the Law, before they were lost in battle. In front of this room, the holy of holies, was the "holy place," where reminders of God's special protection of the Jews were located: the seven-branched candlesticks, Aaron's rod, and the twelve round, flat loaves of bread reminding the people of the manna from heaven which had fed the twelve tribes in the desert.

Jesus would never have been inside that part, of course. He did not belong to a priestly family, being a member of the tribe of Jacob and not of Levi. The whole nation of Jews, however, was priestly. Everyone was terribly interested in the morning and evening sacrifices offered to the Lord by the priests of Aaron's line. The holier an individual Jew was, the more he cared about what went on in the temple. And Jesus was the holiest of Jews!

On the day he made such a commotion in the temple area about the changing of money for profit, he called the buildings "my Father's house." (John 2:16) He loved the temple dearly, yet he knew it would not remain standing very long. During his public career it had already been under construction for forty-six years. Another forty-one or two and down it would come—ruined by the Romans in 70 A.D.

Although Jesus could foresee this destruction, it was not that which he meant to prophesy the day he said, "Destroy this temple, and in three days I will raise it up." (John 2:19) No, he was speaking of the temple of his body. The risen body of Jesus would be the new sanctuary for all to worship before. When it would be taken up in the glory of his ascension, it would become the focal point of all human prayer.

Jesus became not only our temple, but our high priest as well. By his ascension, he went behind the veil of the heavens (as Israel's high priest went behind the temple veil), not once a year, but once only. His prayer to the Father upon his arrival in heaven was a perfect one, because he had completed the work he came on earth to do. Jerusalem's temple found its fulfillment in the temple of the Lord's body.

All these things we must know if we are going to understand Jesus' feelings toward Jerusalem. At the end of his young life, this strong, self-controlled man who had lived in the outdoors for a couple of years cried—actually cried—over the city he loved so much. "Jerusalem, Jerusalem!" he said. "The city that murders the prophets and stones the messengers sent to her. How often would I have gathered your children as a hen gathers her young under her wings; but you would not have it. Behold your house [did he mean your temple?] you will find abandoned, a prey to desolation." (Matthew 23:37ff.)

It seems fairly clear from these words that Jesus is foretelling the destruction of the city he loved so much. He says, "I've tried—tried with all my strength. But I just can't reach your hearts."

We are getting ahead of our story, though. It is not right to quote Jesus' lament over Jerusalem before he has entered Jerusalem. He has been making his way solemnly southward to Judea to suffer and to die. There are stops along the way: at Jericho to see Zaccheus, at Bethany to visit the Lazarus household, and at the Mount of Olives just east of the city.

Then Jesus instructs two of his friends to unhitch an ass's colt in a nearby village, explaining to the owner, "The Master needs it."

Off the little procession goes, once ready, in the fashion of pilgrims from out of the area entering the holy city. Nowadays when we have important visitors, we meet them at the airport, the dock or the depot. In those times, the Jerusalem residents would go out to the edges of the city to escort the pious travelers in on foot. "Open to me the gates of holiness," they would all sing, "I will enter them and give thanks to the Lord . . . This is the day the Lord has made; let us be glad and rejoice in it." (Psalm 117:19, 24)

These verses are taken from the psalm most commonly used to welcome pilgrims at Passover time. A couple of lines in it are very important to the story of Jesus. The crowds sang out: "Blessed is he who comes in the name of the Lord. We bless you from the house of the Lord." (Psalm 117:26)

That sounds harmless enough. Did not any good Israelite come to Jerusalem "in the name of the Lord"? Why shouldn't this shout go up from the temple court to greet Jesus? But his enemies didn't see things that way. They thought that Jesus was accepting honors that should have been reserved to the Messia alone—certainly not to him. They tried to stop the demonstration, the branches of olive and palm strewn out before Jesus, as the sleepy little long-eared beast moved along bearing its holy burden, the Savior of the world.

"Hosanna (meaning 'Save us!') to the Son of David," the people cried. (Matthew 21:15)

Do you hear what they are saying? Jesus' enemies said angrily. "Rabbi, rebuke your disciples," they ordered. (Luke 19:39) But Jesus said to them, "I tell you that if these people keep silence, the very stones will cry out."

In, in he went to the heart of the city he loved more than any place on earth—knowing that it would destroy him.

Think, for a minute, of the Church in our day with all its people, as if it were a splendid city—Jerusalem, in fact. Now think of the temple in that city as if it were the sacrifice of the

Mass, the holiest of human actions that goes on day and night within the Church. Now think of Jesus as he comes back to earth in triumph—not on an ass's back this time, but riding on the clouds of heaven.

Often asked by his friends—simple fisherfolk who didn't know a great deal of theology—what the signs of the last times would be, and how they might expect his coming at the end of the world, Jesus gave a long and detailed answer in the special language of a part of the Bible called *apocalyptic*. His chief answer to them was: Whenever the Son of Man returns it will be sudden and swift. No one can quite prepare for it. But try. If you are ready at heart, then the great suffering that surrounds all men will not be so great for you.

We shall have more to say about this answer of his in the next chapter.

"When the Son of Man comes, will he find faith on earth?" (Luke 18:8) *You* must answer this question. Is your faith a thing of habit? A thing of school or Sunday Mass-time? Are the dark things that go on in the side streets of the city of God—the pious hypocrisies, the cheap little bargains that go masked as acts of religion—the only things Christ will find when he comes back?

There was a destruction of Jerusalem, once, by Romans who did not understand the holiness of religion. Could there ever be a destruction by the holy God, who knows all about the holiness of religion?

Jesus keeps weeping for us. We in the holy city of the Church still have time to change.

-25-

JESUS TEACHES ABOUT THE LAST DAYS

Every once in a while you read in the newspaper about someone who says the end of the world is coming soon—say in 1985, or this July, or next Thursday. In these days of nuclear stockpiles it would take only one madman at the head of a government to bring about the end—of the planet earth at least; but that is not the kind of thing we mean.

The people who issue statements on the date the world will go up in flames are always "religious" types. They do not issue forecasts or predictions. They utter *prophecies.* Now why on earth should religion be interested in the date when the earth is going to end, whimper or bang? Do these prophets really have a clue, or are they just trying to get their names into the newspapers?

The best way to attack this problem is first to see what a prophet is. A prophet is a man who speaks for God. He addresses men in the name of God. Moses was a prophet. Isaia, that Old Testament writer we quote so often, was another. For us Christians, the last and greatest of the prophets was Jesus of Nazareth.

A true prophet, says the Bible, is a man on whom the Spirit of God rests. Now God is all-holy, so a prophet will be holy. But the real test of a prophet is this: what he teaches in the Lord's name either *is* true, or *will come* true, because God is truth itself. (Deuteronomy 18:15–22)

In applying this test to men who claim to have special, inside information about the end of the world, we ask whether they qualify as prophets. First, are they really holy? Are they well-balanced mentally, not fanatics? Do they love and honor the Scriptures, or do they have the Bible as a sort of disease? Part of sainthood, you know, is being mentally sound. Someone has put it this way: "Holiness is wholeness."

Test number two for your modern prophet is this: is he part of the Church, the "pillar and bulwark of truth" (I Timothy 3:15), as Saint Paul calls it? No one can tell the Holy Spirit what he can do and can't do, of course. That goes without saying. (See Mark 9:37–40). It is absurd to think that he can move only Catholic hearts and speak only through Catholic tongues. He will never speak through other churches, though, if they take positions on Christian matters that go against the Church's teaching. We have Jesus' word that the Spirit of truth will never do this. (See John 16:13). Prophecy is a gift of the Church. The Church has always had prophets. She is very careful to listen when a holy person claims to have a vision or to hear heavenly voices. Her real prophets in every age are, of course, her bishops—by virtue of their teaching office.

But notice this. Even though Jesus is Israel's and the Church's greatest prophet, his disciples could never get him to make a prophecy on the date the world would end! He did give us this important warning: "No pupil is above his teacher." (Matthew 10:24) In other words, watch out for the man who foretells what Jesus would not foretell: "But about that day and hour no one knows, not even the angels in heaven, nor even the Son, but only the Father." (Matthew 24:36)

That is the one important thing we ought to underline in this discussion: although we know that the end of the world is coming, we do not know *when*. Sometimes we see signs along the highway which say, "Prepare to meet thy God," or "Jesus is coming soon." These are good signs, bearing important reminders. They speak the language of the New Testament. They come from a time when the first Christians thought that Jesus would quickly return to them, after only a brief stay with his Father. The trouble is he has been gone for more than nineteen centuries now. He may be gone for thousands more. The right word to describe his coming back to us, therefore, is not "soon" but "swiftly" or "unexpectedly." Whenever it happens, it will take us by surprise.

There is only one thing to fear about the end of the world —or our own death, the end of *our* world. That is, will we have our hearts ready when it comes? Nothing else about it should frighten us.

Every time we receive the body of the Lord, it is God coming to judge us through his Son. He judges us lovingly when he does come. Only if he were to find us in sin would the eucharist be a judgment of "guilty" against us. But God has no desire to find us in sin. He wants to judge us favorably again and again throughout our lives, so that the final judgment will be like all the others: "Enter into the joy of the Lord." (Matthew 25:23) In other words, "Share to the full your master's happiness."

How did we get started on all this talk about the end of the world? Actually it is Jesus himself who launched the topic. The idea comes up in the gospel many times in one form or other. The Master always dodges it, or answers his questioner shortly. Finally, Jesus meets the issue head on. Read the two long passages in the gospel, one in chapter 13 of Saint Mark and the other in chapters 24 and 25 of Saint Matthew, in which our Lord gives a long description of the Last Days.

To understand the gospel on this point we need to know how much the Jews of Jesus' day were influenced by thoughts of the final age of the world. Nowadays, people can hardly be made to think about death. They shudder and say: "It's too gruesome." It is almost impossible in the 1960's to get a conversation started about eternal life. But in those times, anyone who happened to ask in a crowd of pious Jews, "I wonder what the Last Days will be like?" could settle down and listen to a good four-hour discussion.

The trouble with all this talk was that it was a threat to true religion. Instead of dwelling on the *message* of the prophets, the people spent all their time on the *language* of the prophets. Some rabbis taught there would be a thousand years of peace and plenty, for example. Others said ten thousand times ten thousand. The heavens would cave in. The moon would turn to blood. The earth would be consumed by a raging fire, so as to be cleansed by it. The one central and certain fact, however, was that the Lord would win out over all his enemies. Through God's anointed king, this victory would be achieved. All nations of the earth would bow down before the Messia of God. This would all come soon, soon, soon!

You may very well ask how this wild talk got started. Israel had been truly taught by God through Moses and the prophets, had she not? Did God work some of this teaching into Scripture? If so, it seems he was deceiving his chosen people. But that is unthinkable. God cannot deceive. What was the story on all these "prophecies"?

Here are the facts in the case: the Hebrew language is filled with rich figures of speech. That means you have one word doing the work of another, time and again, like "lion" for courage, or "a broken reed" for someone you can't depend on. When some men taught others in writing, as did those Israelites whom the Holy Spirit helped to write down the teachings of the prophets, they did it in the most beautiful poetry imaginable. When they described how the Lord would destroy Jerusalem unless she changed her ways, you could not help knowing she was doomed.

Gradually, as the centuries passed, the people laid more and more stress on the language of the prophets, and less and less on what the prophets were getting at. What was the result? A disease—a real disease in the religious spirit of the people. They began to outdo one another in the tall tales they manufactured about the marvels of the End Time. They substituted apocalyptic writing (all sorts of "revelations") for prophetic.

By the time Jesus came to earth, this business had become a national pastime, like gambling on a lottery or boasting about fishing trips. The dangerous thing about this "prophesying" (guessing, really), was that it was terribly mixed up with the true religion taught by the prophets. It was so mixed up that Jesus spent most of his public life trying to untangle the two ideas. The people never completely succeeded in understanding what the prophets were trying to say because this apocalyptic type of writing got in the way.

Time and again the crowds, and even Jesus' close friends, the Twelve, asked him if the kingdom would come soon. Once in a while, Jesus would use a phrase from a book of prophecy in the Bible. In the main, though, he would not go along with the wild-eyed, popular religious beliefs we have been speaking about. To make sure of this, he wouldn't even use the poetic terms of those biblical books. When people tried to steer him in that direction, he firmly went in another.

True religion for our Lord was something calm and peaceful. It was a thing of the head and the heart—not a bundle of emotions tied up with politics and visions and explosions in the heavens. Jesus did keep saying (or hinting) that the kingdom would be set up soon—indeed, had been set up already. (See Luke 10:9; 17:21). His kingdom, while visible, was simple and silent, and to accept it would require faith. (See Mark 4:26–29). Toward the close of his life, our Lord was again approached on this topic by his friends. He met it squarely. These simple fishermen, who had heard what the rabbis were teaching, asked him what the signs of the Last Times would be, and how they might expect his coming at the end of the world. (Matthew 24:3) Slowly, patiently, he answered. On this occasion *only*, he used the language the Jews had at their command to speak about these things. It was the *language* of the prophets. Using it, he spoke the *message* of the prophets. The return of the Son of Man, he said, will be sudden and swift. No one can be fully ready, but everyone must try to be. If your hearts are ready, said Jesus, then the sufferings that men will experience when God comes to judge will not be so great for you. (You must read Matthew 24 and 25, Mark 13, and Luke 17:26–37 to get the Master's full message).

Are we clear on this matter of the Last Days? Jesus *will*

come back. He will come in splendor. His coming will be unexpected and we must prepare for it, for Jesus will judge us.

The terrible destruction of Jerusalem by the Roman armies, which happened some forty years after Jesus' time, like the sack of that same city by the Babylonians in 587 B.C., gives us some inkling of what God will permit in the way of judgment. What God wants us to think about, though, when we receive his Son in the eucharist, or think about our own death, is how he wants to judge us *in his love.* The joyous sentence of Jesus to be spoken at the judgment is the classic place in Scripture for that: "Come, the elect of my Father! Take possession of the kingdom prepared for you at the beginning of the world." (Matthew 25:34)

THE MASTER TAKES LEAVE OF HIS FRIENDS

Do you know a poem of Shelley's called *Ozymandias of Egypt?* You find it frequently in textbooks of English literature. It's about a man who is trudging across the desert and comes upon a statue that has been standing for centuries. He removes from the base some of the sand that has been covering it, and slowly reads the inscription: "My name is Ozymandias, king of kings: Look on my words, ye Mighty, and despair!"

You see immediately what the poet is getting at. Poor old Ozymandias and his opinion of his own importance. Is *he* ever dead! So are all the kings and emperors and popes who ordered great tombs built over them so that no one would ever forget them. The only ones who live on in human memory, it seems (aside from dictators) are those who serve other people. Statesmen, artists and musicians, for example, leave something behind them–gifts, for all to enjoy.

Actually, the best remembered men are the saints–those heroes of unselfishness who forget their way into the remembrance of everyone who comes after them.

The moral seems to be, "If you want to be forgotten, remember yourself; and if you want to be remembered, forget yourself."

Throughout these pages, we find ourselves discussing Jesus of Nazareth. He is Israel's Messia. He has a higher title still. He is the Lord. The earliest act of faith made in him by Christians describes him as "both Lord and Christ." (Saint Peter said that in Acts 2:36). An important question to ask about him is this: in what sense does he still live on in the world? Some people who do not believe Jesus is the Son of God say that we Christians have just decided to keep on saying forever how wonderful it was that he died for our sins. The fact is, however (these people say), that Jesus was only a man. He lives on only in our memories, not in glory at the right hand of God the Father.

The honest believer needs to ask himself, "Does Jesus still live or is he like Ozymandias, except that men have buried him under a different pile of sand? Have they just decided to honor him as God?"

Some Christians experience this difficulty on their own. Every Christian needs to face it. It would be plain foolishness to raise every question about Jesus except the really big one. That question is not, "Who *was* he?" but "Who *is* he?" Who is he to me? Today. In my life. Is he a character in history whose words and deeds we remember admiringly, or is he someone living and acting *now* in the world right outside the door? Does he still have all the power of God he showed when he lived in the land of Israel and among its people, or is he a great teacher from the past?

Jesus is the King of time. Jesus is the Lord of history. All the ages lie open before him as if they were a single moment. The weaver's apprentice of fourteenth century France and the businessman of Stockholm in the twenty-second century are present to him just as truly as his mother Mary was present to him in their home at Nazareth, although in a different way. Ever since his return to heaven from which he came, he has been alive and active to save us. He is ever-present to his Father and ever-present to us. He rules over us from his place of honor at the Father's right hand; the way he does it is by being the Servant of us all. He is ever-living, to make intercession for us. (Hebrews 7:25) He has entered into heaven itself, "where he now presents himself in the presence of God on our behalf." (Hebrews 9:24)

The worst mistake we could make about Jesus would be to think of him as someone out of the past. The gospel was written because the early Christians who hadn't known him in life wanted a record of his words and deeds. But the first way they came to know him was to meet him every day in his brothers in the community of love they called "the Church." They met him in the sacraments they received, especially the meal of celebration that contained him, the eucharist. The chief thing the eucharist did for them is what it does for us, namely form a community of charity.

Christ was active in each one of these holy signs—in baptism, in confirmation, in the eucharist—by uniting himself to all those who received them in a spirit of faith. During his earthly days, he approached people as individuals, not just in a crowd. He always came to them as a friend. He was never high-and-mighty, never looking for reasons to scold or blame, always open in his manner and deeply interested in people on a man-to-man basis.

When he comes to us in the Church through the holy sacraments, he always comes in that same spirit.

The one thing that sets Jesus apart from the heroes and saints of all the ages is that he is not the prisoner of time. He is not someone (like poor Ozymandias) who once had influence but has it no more. He has won out over the centuries and over distances and over death. In a word, he *is*, because the Father has raised him up in glory. Because he exists forever as the "image of God" (II Corinthians 4:4), Jesus is a special person, an individual, to a multitude of men.

That is the faith in him that you and I have through the Church. That is the faith in him that the gospel is a reminder of. He does not simply speak to us out of a book of writings. He speaks to us in a living community of people (the Church) who reflect his love in their lives, who "belong to Christ, and Christ to God." (I Corinthians 3:23)

We are constantly quoting in these pages the words of Holy Scripture. The Bible is God's message from heaven to men. All of the books that go to make it up are the written record of a spoken Word, the Word God speaks to us through his Son. In fact, his Son *is* that Word. God's message to us and his only Son whom he sends to save us are one and the same. After Jesus, the eternal Word of God, went back to his Father, he continues to speak to us through his Church.

There you have the simple truth of how God speaks to his sons. It is a very important matter to grasp. We need to treasure it for a lifetime. There is a single Word of God, you see, and that is Christ. God speaks to us through this Word each time the Church celebrates a sacrament. The men who have faith in Christ hear God speak every time they receive a sacrament, but in the eucharist most of all.

God speaks to us through the Bible, too, particularly the New Testament. When the two go together, for example when a long and beautiful part of the Bible is read at Mass, or when a couple gets married, or a sick person is anointed, and the Bible is read as part of the ceremony, you have God speaking to his people. He does it in two ways: in a sign that you see, or taste, or touch—the sacraments—(for example, the living body of the Lord), and a sign you hear—the Scriptures. Jesus is the whole content of this twofold message. God "says" Christ to us; that is the Word he utters. He wants us to answer by saying "Amen," that is, "I believe," once we have heard this Word spoken.

Is it safe to assume that you're going to let God speak to you for the rest of your life? Let's hope so. The chief occasion to hear him is when you offer Christ to the Father in the eucharist and receive him back again as your food. Penance is another time when God will speak to you through Christ—then at your marriage, or your priestly ordination, or when you are anointed in illness.

But God can better "get through" to you in these sacraments if you are constantly reading the Scriptures as well, to learn what Jesus intends the sacraments to do for you. That New Testament of yours—the gospel especially—should be so well thumbed by the time you die that everyone will be able to say: "He let God try to speak to him through the holy sacraments." That is what happens any time we open the gospel, even at random. God speaks to our hearts. Then we hear his words proclaimed in the Mass. Finally, we walk forward to the holy table and let God speak his perfect Word, his Son, to us in the eucharistic gifts.

A most important section of the gospel of Christ is that series of four chapters according to Saint John numbered 14 through 17. There the Lord Jesus speaks at length to his friends at the Last Supper. You should read it often. It is a very good way to be put in touch with the spirit of the Master. The whole fourth gospel–Saint John's–is written in such a way that anywhere you open it you meet the whole person of Jesus in his ideas and his words. It's like sawing the trunk of a tree at any point: a good clear cut gives you its whole life history in the rings. In the same way, any part of the gospel–but these four chapters in particular–gives you the whole Jesus, Son of God and Son of Man.

"A new commandment I give you: love one another; as I love you, so I want you, too, to love one another." (John 13:34. The old commandment on this point is in Leviticus 19:18. Look it up and tell how this one is new). "This is what will prove to all men you are my disciples," Jesus continues, "your love one for another." (John 13:35)

Why must Jesus leave his disciples? Remember, they have never succeeded in understanding that Jesus must suffer and die, even though he has tried to explain this to them several times. His answer on his need to depart is: "I am going to prepare a place for you . . . then I shall come back and take you home with me. I want you to be where I shall be." (John 14:2–4)

These followers of his must spend years and years (and you and I our entire lifetimes), living apart from the daily impact of his personality that had changed their lives so completely. How would they be equal to the separation? How will we? He answers that although he is going back to the Father and to his own glory, it is only by going back that the Spirit of truth will be given to them. "And should you ask for anything in my name I will do it, that the Father may be glorified in the Son." (John 14:13–16) This promise sounds like one of those wild promises in a chain letter until you read on a bit and see what type of favor Jesus is interested in granting. His big interest, notice, is that the Father shall be praised by men. This praise or glory will be given *in* the Son. If the friends of Jesus love him, he tells them, they will obey the commandments he gives them. When they do, Jesus will ask the Father, "and he will grant you another Advocate to be with you for all time to come: the Spirit of truth." (John 14:16)

It is in the Spirit that these words of God spoken in the gospel, spoken in the Church by Jesus, head of the Church, go on and on. They are like a brilliant cascade or waterfall. Every droplet, every gushing jet strikes the sun at a new angle and increases the beauty of the whole. *As we grow in God's grace, these phrases in the gospel grow in meaning for us.* They are signs of the never-ending presence of Jesus in our midst as the Church of God. We are his holy people gathered before him. We have the great sacrament of his body and blood, and the other "sacrament" of his spoken word in the gospel. *Neither sign can do its full work of grace in us without the other*.

See, you must love me, Christ says, I who have first loved you. Then prove your love. I am the roadway: walk on me. I am the truth: believe me. I am life: live by me. If you do this my Father will have to love you. He cannot fail to, being a God of love. Then he and I will send the Holy Spirit to be your friend. The Spirit will make everything plain to you and recall to your minds everything I have told you.

"I have told you this that my joy may be yours, and your hearts may be brimful of joy." (John 15:11)

Those who love us and have some authority over us give us advice. When this advice is about a good and holy life it is sometimes called "good counsel." To follow this advice is right, but it should be made very clear that this is not enough. If you want to live a *full Christian life,* you should let the Father speak to you in Jesus Christ's words and follow the "interior Master," the Holy Spirit. That is the way that

Father, Son and Holy Spirit will come to you and dwell within you.

Jesus left his friends only so that he could come back to them for all time in those two great signs of grace, his eucharistic body and the holy scriptures.

–27–

THE LAST SUPPER: VOW AND REMEMBRANCE RITE

In the preceding chapter we spoke about Jesus' words of comfort and instruction to his twelve friends at their last supper together, the night before he left them to suffer and die. It was perfectly natural that he should be eating with them in Jerusalem at this time of year. The time was spring, the season of the Passover or great Jewish feast of remembrance. The chief thing the people called to mind on this occasion was the deliverance of Israel by her God, the Lord, centuries earlier (thirteen centuries is about as close as we can come; the event is described in chapter 12 of Exodus, but there are no clear chronological indications there).

From the gospels we cannot learn the exact year of Jesus' crucifixion. The best conclusion is that our Lord's last earthly Passover came in early April of 30 A.D. This date is based on what little the gospels tell us about the length of Jesus' public life, and calendar indications which tell us in what year the fourteenth day of Nisan, the day of Passover, fell on Friday. Other years that have been suggested, in the order of their likelihood, are: 33, 29, 31, 28 and 32. Complicated, wouldn't you say?

This variety of opinions, however, tells us something important about the gospels. Matthew, Mark, Luke and John—the four inspired writers—had no interest in such matters as dates, but they did have a burning interest in how this Passover was the last and perfect one. They cared greatly that it was a sign of the deliverance Jesus would be interceding for, at the Father's right hand, as long as men had need of it.

The gospel account is full of unsolved problems of detail about the Last Supper. For instance, the meal is nowhere described in so many words as being a Jewish Passover meal. All the emphasis is on the fact that it is a *new* Pasch (a word taken from the Greek form of the Hebrew *pesach,* a *sparing* or *exemption*). We must conclude that the only fitting time for Jesus to celebrate this new and perfect remembrance meal was on the occasion of the old meal that had pointed to it for so long.

"When the hour had come," writes Saint Luke, "he took his place on a couch, and so did the apostles. 'It has been my heart's desire,' he said to them, 'to eat this paschal supper with you before I suffer. I tell you, I shall not eat it again till it is fulfilled in the kingdom of God.'" (Luke 22:14–16)

See how anxious Jesus is that this celebration should take place among them as a family group. Even Judas, the black sheep of the "little flock" (Luke 12:32), is there. Notice, too, the relation between the joyous celebration and the bitter death that will follow it. This is somewhat like the happy Thanksgiving dinner of a condemned man with his family on the night before he is to be hanged. In the gospel case, however, the relation between the two events is not just one of before-and-after, or even of a gathering on the eve of tragedy, arranged to provide a happy memory for family and friends.

No, Jesus' meaning goes much deeper than that. He is saying that this supper has a certain finality about it. It is closely related to the coming of God's kingdom, in the way that a sign is to the thing it stands for. Like a prophet of old, Jesus utters a solemn vow that he will touch no food until something very important happens. Meanwhile, he will drink of *this cup* and eat of *this bread* to hasten the event which he foretells—the coming of the kingdom.

At this point time out should be taken to read the gospel account of the Last Supper; it is almost useless to go on exploring this topic without this background. Luke's account (22:7–38) and Matthew's account (26:20–29) should be read first, then Mark 14:12–25 and I Corinthians 11:23–25.

What are the main things to single out in this event? There

have been preparations made for the meal, of course. On the first of eight days when the Jews ate all of their bread free of yeast—a holdover from an ancient Spring agricultural festival —Peter and John are sent by the Master to get things ready. All over Jerusalem, pilgrims are eating this meal as families or groups of families in dining rooms. Chapter 12 of Exodus gives you a description of how they had to roast the lamb and prepare the yeast-free bread and bitter herbs for the paschal supper.

The upstairs room which Peter and John arranged for is "spacious and well furnished." (Luke 22:12) The thirteen husky men—all outdoor types, at least during the last few years—mount to the dining place, probably by way of an outside stairway. There they "lie down to eat." (Matthew 26:20; Mark 14:17) The Jews had adopted the Greek custom of reclining at the table for banquets.

The most painful part seems to come early in the meal. Jesus has already said clearly that he expects to die before long. (Matthew 26:2; Mark 14:8) Now he makes a direct reference to how it will happen: "Frankly I tell you, one of you will betray me." (Matthew 26:21) The various accounts describe how Jesus told Judas in different ways that he knew he was the guilty one. There must have been a great hubbub of voices at the table. Surely by now the men had heard how the leading priests were sworn to "get" Jesus. Whether all, or Judas only, heard our Lord's words to Judas we cannot tell; but Judas certainly heard them. Saint Matthew makes the direct accusation spoken by Jesus very clear. "It is not I, is it, Rabbi?" Judas asks. (Matthew 26:25) Jesus replies that the words are his, a Jewish way of saying, "Now that you've said it, make of it what you will."

Notice that there is a sign here at the table ("Jesus answered, 'It is he to whom I will give the morsel, after dipping it in the bowl.' So he dipped the morsel, and with his own hand reached it to Judas Iscariot, the son of Simon." John 13:26) There will likewise be a sign later in the garden. ("And when he came, he [Judas] went straight up to him, and said, 'Rabbi!' and kissed him." Mark 14:45) This time the sign is food shared in common (Matthew 26:23); later it will be a warm embrace. (Luke 22:48) It is especially fitting that a betrayal should have the same signs as a friendship. You cannot describe sin any better than by saying that it is selling out a friend—trading on a close relationship for private gain.

The central event at the supper is the blessing Jesus pronounces over the bread and wine. When we read the account carefully and slowly, we can see that his words are in a fixed form (actually, in four fixed forms). The essentials are there in all four cases. They are very much like the fixed form of words used by the priest at the consecration of the Mass. This should not surprise us. We ought to expect it. Saint Paul says that he learned what Jesus said and did at the supper table "from the Lord" (I Corinthians 11:23), that is to say—as scholars understand him to mean—from the community at Jerusalem whose living tradition is, in fact, the voice of "the Lord."

Jesus' words and actions seem abrupt and business-like; there is no wasted motion or speech. This is because these phrases are already worn smooth with usage, like the stones in a river bed. They are taken from the community celebration of this sacred meal by Christians in Palestine, Rome and Antioch (where the first three gospels were composed). The eucharistic meal is already decades old when the gospel accounts of it come to be written.

In each account, Jesus takes the bread, speaks a blessing in praise of God over it, breaks it and hands it around: "Take! Eat! This is my body." He does the same with the cup of wine. As he passes this around, his words to his friends are different, naturally: "Drink of it, every one of you; for this is my covenant-blood, which is about to be shed for the sake of many, with a view to the forgiveness of sins. I tell you, I shall never drink again of the product of the vine till that day when I drink new wine with you in the kingdom of my Father." (Matthew 26:28–29)

We may wonder why Jesus spoke and acted as he did. Did his friends understand him? They were probably mystified, we may surmise, but they had a few clues. First of all, the idea of a sacred meal is as old as the people Israel. The Passover feast was the one best known; but in Jesus' day, pious groups were meeting all the time to take part in holy actions like this. They first said grace—a prayer of thanks to the Creator for his gifts of food and drink. Their thanks was not an ordinary "Thanks," however. Indeed not. The form they used was that of first reciting the marvelous deeds done by God in the past to save his people; then his holy name was blessed in gratitude for these deeds of his.

This is what Jesus did. This is what we do in the Mass. First we review all that God has done for us, in the *preface.* Then we bring that great blessing in praise of God to a climax by the priest's words which change food and drink into our gift to God, the living body and blood of Jesus.

At the last supper, our Lord did exactly what you would expect—up to a point. He presided over a family meal, passing the food around after he blessed it. The chief items that received a blessing were bread and wine, signs for the Jews of all food and drink. Then Jesus indicated that the new Passover bread that they were to eat as an *everlasting* remembrance was the bread of his body, not the yeast-free bread they ate at the old remembrance meal. They were no longer merely to recall the deliverance from Egypt under Moses, but the deliverance from sin under Jesus. This was a major change. Moses had given them manna, bread from the heavens to keep them from starving. (Exodus 16:8–35) Jesus gave them himself to eat as their food for the same purpose.

Secondly, Jesus drew up an agreement with the whole human race and used his blood as the sign of it. This is what Moses had done when he gave the people the Ten Commandments and the Book of the Law. He sprinkled the people with the blood of bulls to prove how faithful God was going to be to the agreement, and how faithful the people ought to be. (Exodus 24:1–8) At the supper, Jesus said that this covenant-blood of his, now no longer wine, was going to be shed as a part of a new and everlasting agreement. It would not only be the *sign* of setting men free from their sins. It would actually *cause* this to happen. They were to be sons of the covenant (*b'nai b'rith,* you would say in Hebrew), sons of this new and eternal agreement between God and all his children. It was sealed not in the blood of bulls and heifers but in the blood of Jesus Christ. (Read chapter 9 of the Epistle to the Hebrews right now. You will find it hard, but when you get to verse 18 it will begin to look familiar).

Once Jesus passes his body and blood around to be eaten and drunk, they chant the final hymn of praise and go out into the night. He is to offer himself to God now, as a victim for men's sins. He will die a painful death, marked by bloodshed. It will come as a result of his perfect love for the Father and for us. The comforting thought about this death is this: *it will make the eucharist—the sign of Christ's love—available to us always.*

That is why the Church constantly invites us to step forward to the table and eat. She does what Jesus does. Christians are those who follow their bishop, or the priest he sends them, in performing this act of love in the bread and in the cup. To be Catholic is to belong to that worldwide holy communion which the eucharist creates. It is to receive life from Christ's body, remission of sins from his blood.

Might you ever wish to stop taking this meal? You're free to, you know. Judas walked out on it. "And it was night," the gospel says. (John 13:30) Remember that from time to time. You may leave the feast whenever you please; but it is "night."

–28–

AGONY AND TRIAL
"I AM HE"

Every man who lives on this earth has to die. This is the price of sin that all of us must pay. Some people die gallantly; others badly. Many die in pain. Some die without any idea that death is overtaking them. Though many die happy deaths, no one can be said to die with pleasure. Peace marks the death of the man with a good conscience who believes that he will rise again. Yet every normal human being shrinks from death because it is an unknown experience.

Jesus shrank from death. He knew he was to overcome death forever within a matter of days. Even so, as he lay outstretched on the ground in prayer, in the olive grove where he went after the Last Supper, he shuddered at the prospect of death.

We cannot say that it was death alone that frightened Jesus. He was to die as a result of the evil in his enemies' hearts. That knowledge would have been a shock to someone whose heart was full of love, as his was. Much worse, Jesus was to die under the weight of the sins of all men everywhere. This was a tremendous burden. He must have recoiled at the thought of being so closely associated with sin, he who was without sin.

Or—and this last suggestion is not to be dismissed lightly—being the most intelligent and sensitive of men, Jesus may have been in mortal dread of the pain that lay ahead for him. This wouldn't mean he was not brave—far from it. Rather, it would have required a special bravery for one so sensitive as he to face his brutal death.

It is hard to know Jesus' innermost thoughts, but it is not hard at all to know his words. "Abba" (Aramaic for Father), he said, "You can do all things! Spare me this cup! No, not what I will, but what you will." (Mark 14:36)

The English word *agony* comes from the Greek word for a contest, like that of wrestlers. The agony Jesus suffered in the Garden of Gethsemane was a death-struggle with the forces of evil. He went out to the slope of the Mount of Olives, directly east of Jerusalem, with his friends. There were only eleven of them, now that Judas had deserted. The Passover moon was close to full. Despite its light, this was soon to be the hour of the power of darkness. (See Luke 22:53).

Jesus felt he had to warn his friends about the weakness that would overtake them. "You will all stumble and fall," was the sense of what he told them. (See Mark 14:27). Then he quoted a prophet of old, Zacharia, to this effect: "I will smite the shepherd, and the sheep will be scattered." (See Zacharia 13:7). Just as the whole nation Israel, made up of twelve tribes, had suffered from lack of leadership many times, so this little group of friends would run like frightened sheep once Jesus was taken from them.

He was right in his prophecy, of course. He knew their anxious hearts—and he knew that the Holy Spirit had not yet come to strengthen them. The eleven were to prove about as spineless and unintelligent as you and I would be if we were to turn away from the leadership of Christ. Have you ever thought of that—what a "nothing" each of us would be on his own, without Jesus as our Head?

Peter—poor, excitable Peter—got all worked up over this. Everybody desert the Teacher? No sir, not he! (See Mark 14:29). Then Jesus had to give Peter the facts about his weakness. Before the hour of 5:30 or 6:00 A.M. (second cockcrow, as they called it), Peter would have proved himself to be a weakling. Three different times he would swear to high heaven that he had never met Jesus. That is what Jesus told Peter would happen, but Peter denied it with all his strength—said he would sooner die than do that.

All the rest of them said the same thing. In a way, the

other ten were right in saying they wouldn't deny him. They didn't stay close enough to Jesus to be heard saying *anything* about him!

Then, the three who were closest to Jesus—Peter, James and John—went to sleep on the job! The Passover meal was a big one; at least four cups of wine were required as part of it. You've guessed what happened. While Jesus was going through the bitterest struggle his soul had ever faced, his three friends went sound asleep. When he came back and found them, he called Peter by his given name, Simon. Peter was no "rock" now, the meaning of the name Peter (or Kepha, as Jesus would have called him in their own language). He was no better than a handful of pebbles.

Twice more Jesus came back, and twice more he found them dead to the world. Fine thing! Satan could have brought the kingdom of God to the brink of destruction (never destroyed it, of course), and this trio would still be snoring away. The difference between the devil and those who declare themselves friends of God is summed up in this scene, somehow. Satan doesn't sleep. It's a good thing Jesus doesn't either, or we'd have gone under a long time ago, for *we* sleep. Our lives as strong friends at the Master's side can be called one long cat nap.

On his third return to the sleeping disciples, Jesus roused them by saying that the hour had come for the Son of Man to be betrayed. When he used the word *hour,* he did not mean sixty minutes but that period of climax when the world would be saved by his death and resurrection. At the beginning of his career—at Cana, when a sign was asked for—Jesus made it clear that his hour had not yet come. (John 2:4) Now he was equally clear in stating that it had come.

In a darker sense, Judas' hour had come, too. Out he came, at the head of an armed band, to the place of Christ's prayer, a place he knew well.

It is hard to know from the gospel exactly who these armed men were; probably temple police. It is perfectly clear whom they represented, namely Jesus' sworn enemies among the leading priests and learned men and elders.

"Who is it you are looking for?" Jesus asked.

"Jesus of Nazareth," they answered.

Jesus said to them, "I am he." (John 18:5–6) At that moment, they fell back and dropped to the ground. That "I am" (the exact wording of Jesus' answer) terrified them, for it was the very name that God had used to identify himself when he spoke to Moses at the burning bush. (Exodus 3:14)

Almost everyone has heard how our Lord reacted to Judas' warm embrace, the signal that this was the one they were looking for. Jesus called Judas "friend" and asked him what business he had come on. Not that Jesus needed to know. It was the kind of question that was meant to slow down the onrush of evil by getting the sinner to pause and look within himself. But it didn't work. "Rabbi," Judas said, and kissed Jesus. "And they seized him and held him." (Mark 14:45)

Simon Peter put up a brief fight by swinging his sword at a servant of the high priest, a certain Malchus. Peter managed to cut off the servant's right ear. Saint Luke, author of the "gospel of healing" as the third gospel is sometimes called, says that Jesus restored the ear miraculously with a touch. (Luke 22:51)

The Master then looked squarely at this band of hired thugs with their swords and clubs, and spoke to them as his ancestor David had spoken to Goliath. Just as David's confidence had been in the Lord and not in a suit of armor, so Jesus' trust was wholly in his Father. He had no fear whatever of strong-arm tactics. He had taught daily in the temple and in the streets. (Luke 22:53) No one had captured him then. They needed the cover of night for their dirty business. They required the confusion of a busy feast day to mask their deed.

A verse occurs in Scripture at this point which may be the most pathetic in all the Bible: "Then all his disciples left him and fled." (Mark 14:50)

Life is full of mysteries. One of the greatest is why supposedly religious people fall apart in a time of crisis. It happens all the time. It happened then; it is happening now, in high schools, in the armed forces all over the world, in colleges, in big cities, in residential neighborhoods. Should anyone ask you: "If you were with Jesus then, would you have left him?" your immediate response would be, "Of course not." But isn't that what happens when anyone chooses to leave his Church to marry someone he thinks he can't live without? when he collapses morally while on overseas duty, or takes his first payoff in a job of public trust?

How does this happen? The Catholic cannot say that the Spirit hasn't come upon him as yet, as one can say of the apostles; most have been confirmed, in fact. When individuals do abandon Christ, this shows that the descent of the Spirit upon them hasn't meant much to them. It shows that their confirmation was chiefly a catechism bee, not a being set on fire by the Strengthener of hearts.

Secondly, it's evident that following Jesus has never yet cost these deserters anything. A little inconvenience, perhaps, but no more. When they reach a test, the first real test, and do not choose Christ, it is because he doesn't mean anything to them. Or if he means something, he doesn't mean enough. When Jesus isn't a person in your life whom you know as a friend, turning and running makes sense. Who wants to die, after all, or miss out on the only kicks available, for someone he doesn't even *know?*

The mystery of our redemption, though, is a mystery of God's love, not of man's weakness. For that reason we should never use the gospel as a mere occasion for lessons on moral conduct. Our thoughts must always rise higher than the level of our weak natures. The gospel speaks in part of the mystery of sin, but it speaks much more of the mystery of Christ who alone can overcome sin. We examine our defeats only so that the victory of Christ may mean strength to us.

Jesus showed his strength and self-possession to the priests and the elders first. (Mark 14:53–65; John 18:12–27) The high priest Annas got Jesus to admit he was the Messia, the Son of "the Blessed One." In the previous decades, many Jews had claimed to be the Messia. It was not an evil claim to make. But to be God's Son, in terms of special closeness, Annas called this blasphemy. Jesus went right ahead with his claim. He had to speak the truth even though it would cost him his life.

Even while Peter was denying him before a servant girl in the courtyard, Jesus was being shipped off to Pilate. This Roman governor (*procurator* was his Roman title) hated the Jews whom he ruled over. He caught on to their game quickly and started trying to find ways to set Jesus free. (Luke 23:1–25; John 18:28–19:16) He began to probe into who Jesus thought he was. The deeper Pilate probed, the more frightened he became. Finally, like a man yielding to panic who murders a witness to silence him, Pilate released Jesus to die. He feared being reported in Rome, and when the leaders threatened to turn him in for not protecting Caesar's interests he turned to jelly. (John 19:12) Jesus had never threatened the empire or Caesar for a minute, but Pilate acted in haste and out of fear. He crumpled, and the trial was over.

Was it Pilate who was guilty of Jesus' death? Was it Israel's leaders? the Jerusalem mobs? The Church gives a short and simple answer to this tangled question. She says, "It was our sins." That is where the guilt *surely* lies.

As to the various persons in the gospel, only God knows their hearts, and what he knows he does not tell.

–29–

JESUS DIES BECAUSE HIS WORK IS FINISHED

There is a story told about Marshal Lyautey, the French resident general of Morocco before and after World War I, that describes his hurry to get things done. One morning under the bright North African sun, he told the orderly landscaping his compound that, by noon, he wanted a certain plant moved from one place to another. The orderly was too heavy for light work, so he raised an objection that was a stroke of genius. "What's the hurry, *mon Général?*" he asked. "After all, it's a century plant and it won't bloom for another eighty years." "Then," Lyautey answered, "we haven't a moment to lose!"

Jesus of Nazareth, too, went about his public career like a man who hadn't a moment to lose. He was never rushed, never feverish in his activity; yet he lost no time in accomplishing his task. Once when he wanted to go back to Judea, the southern province where Jerusalem lay, his friends objected because they feared for his safety. Earlier he had met his bitterest opposition there. This time, the disciples were afraid that he might not escape with his life. "Rabbi, only recently the Jews [Judeans?] wanted to stone you to death," they said, "and you mean to go back there again?"

Jesus answered: "Are there not twelve hours to the day? As long as a man walks in the day, he does not stumble because he sees the light of this world. But when a man walks in the night he stumbles because he has no light to guide him." (John 11:8–10)

This is Jesus' way of telling us of the importance of an opportunity sent by God. In his case, there is a job to do in saving the world. The Father has appointed the time in which to do it, included the amount of time which Jesus has to accomplish it. Saint John makes an important play on words in this passage. He takes the simple statement of Jesus about daylight and dark (there was no electricity or gas in those days, remember) and reports a powerful reference that Jesus made to himself. Jesus is the Light of this world. The forces of evil and refusal to believe in him are darkness. Not only is Jesus' lifetime before he is captured *his* unique opportunity; it is also the opportunity of *everyone* who would walk in his light. Jesus used this providential time to do the work the Father had sent him to do, and when his hour had come he died on the cross to free us from the guilt of our sins.

The image of Christ on the cross, which is used so often to recall this task that Jesus accomplished, might give the impression that Jesus' followers are deeply concerned with torture and bloodshed. Actually, *Christianity is a religion of hope and joy*. If that is so, why is the cross our great sign? The answer is that even though Jesus' death *is only the first stage* of the mystery of our redemption, *it is the part that best reminds us of his love*.

The crucifix wasn't used as a sign of the way God saved us until Christianity was at least five centuries old. The holy eucharist is the oldest and best sign of our salvation. That is why Jesus gave it to us, to act as a sign which would save us.

Before the crucifix gained favor as a sign of our salvation, a cross set with precious stones was used, to show that Jesus is the world's rich treasure. His glorious wounds are like gems to us. (In fact, the custom of covering the crucifix with violet during Passiontide started with the covering of these precious gems—not the image of Christ's body).

However, an image of Christ standing glorious beside an empty tomb, or ascending to his Father, would remind us of our redemption just as well as the crucifix does. The crucifix especially helps us to recall the *pain* or *cost* of the great mystery of the redemption, whereas picturing Christ's glory following his death aids us in remembering the Father's *acceptance* or *approval* of this redemption of mankind.

A complete reminder of the mystery by which God saves

us can be seen in three wood carvings which hang above the altars of a church dedicated to Saint Pius X in Aurora, Colorado. On the gospel side you see Mary holding up her infant Son, who is wrapped in swaddling bands which are painted silver. The center carving is of Christ crucified; this time he is clad in the loincloth of his last hours. On the epistle side you see Jesus coming forth from his tomb, with his linen gravecloth a silver sheen behind him as he goes heavenward.

This full story of the redemption is a far better reminder than the devotion of the Way of the Cross, which stops when the story is half over. Indeed, there are special reasons why showing Christ in kingly robes or in priestly vestments is better than showing his naked, bleeding body. Again, that is because we are reminded of the whole mystery when we see Christ in his glory, and not just a part of it as in a crucifixion scene; for Christ is not death to us—but life! His dying on the cross reminds us of our sins, it is true, for Satan is still victorious over Jesus at this point. But when Jesus rises from the dead in priestly glory, he reminds us that he has crushed the serpent's head (defeated Satan) and washed away all the guilt of our sins.

Jesus himself said, when he referred to himself as the good shepherd, that no one could rob him of his life: "I have power to lay it down and power to take it back again." (John 10:18) The Father's will governed when and how this should happen.

At the Last Supper, Jesus raised his eyes to heaven and said, "Father, the hour is come." (John 17:1) Then he prayed, asking God for glory so that he in turn might glorify the Father: "I have glorified you on earth by completing the work you gave me to do . . . I have made your name known to the men whom you singled out from the world and entrusted to me . . . the message you delivered to me I have delivered to them." (John 17:4, 6, 8) Every word Jesus spoke breathed certainty that he had faithfully carried out the mission on which he had been sent. So his death was not untimely, nor a moment too soon. It came at exactly the right time, because his work was finished.

The way his death came about was swift and sickening. You must know the story. Pilate had tried hard to excite some pity in the crowd for Jesus, but it didn't work. He called Jesus "king of the Jews" at one point. Now this was a bad mistake, for the Jewish people never used this title because they knew their own history well enough to realize that only the Lord was king over Israel. Was Pilate taunting them, they wondered?

Then, when he offered to free either the prisoner Barabbas or Jesus (as was the custom on religious feasts), Pilate proved how little he knew about the political situation. Here this thug, Barabbas, was in prison for murder and revolt against Roman rule, while Jesus, who proved by his miracles that he had the power to do something to win Israel's independence, hadn't raised a finger. For the mob, bent on rebellion against Rome with the dagger and a curse, this was no choice at all. "Barabbas!" they cried. Give us our own kind, in other words.

Pilate tried one thing more. He had Jesus whipped. (John 19:1) Neither that, nor the cruel game of the soldiers in the courtyard in which they mocked Jesus as a king, had any effect. The crowd wanted blood. Pilate had more weakness than pity in his make-up, so he gave in and turned Jesus over to be crucified.

In those days the condemned man had to carry his own crossbeam, a rough-hewn affair, to the place of execution.* Someone helped Jesus on his way to be crucified—a man named Simon. He was "drafted" into helping Jesus, the gos-

* The Greek word for the heavy crossbeam that Jesus had to carry is *stauros*. This is a Christian name in Russia—Stavros; occasionally you read of a Communist diplomat with that name. That is a case of bearing Christ's cross whether you want to or not. There surely ought to be hope for a man like that, or an Anastas, "resurrection"; Vassily, "king"; Nikita, "victory"—all names taken from the mystery of Christ.

pel says. (Mark 15:21) The gospel also says that Jesus met good women on his way who wailed over his death.

He was dragged to the knob of sandstone outside Jerusalem where criminals were put to death in those days. It was called *Golgotha,* "place of the skull." (Matthew 27:33) "Calvary" says the same thing in Latin. Perhaps it was called that because of the remains of other crucifixions at the place. Grisly business!

Have you ever seen a skull at the bottom of a cross? Sometimes the crucifix on a rosary will have one. It goes back to an old Christian legend that Adam was buried where Christ gave his life. That theory isn't much good as history, but as theology it's hard to improve on. What Adam lost for us, Christ regained. The father of death, Adam, lies at the feet of the first Victor over death, Christ Jesus.

Jesus was crucified between two robbers. Saint Mark says he was crucified between the "wicked." (Mark 15:28) This is a powerful reference to one of the Servant Songs we spoke of earlier: "And he was counted among the wicked." (Isaia 53:12) The earth grew dark: "It was now the sixth hour, and there was darkness over the whole land until the ninth hour." (Luke 23:44) Men shrieked at Jesus and challenged him to come down: "He saved others, himself he cannot save. If he is the king of Israel, let him come down now from the cross, and we will believe him." (Matthew 27:42) A thief asked forgiveness: "Lord, remember me when you come into your kingdom." (Luke 23:42) Jesus spoke gently to his mother: "Woman, behold, your son." (John 19:26), and we begin to see why he addressed her in this way at Cana. (John 2:4) He gave her, the new Eve, as mother to us all.

Mostly, though, Jesus went on with his dying. He had a work to do. Nothing would keep him from it.

Jesus cried out loudly. All that the crowds could hear was a snatch of a psalm: "O God, my God, look upon me: why have you forsaken me?" (Psalm 21:2. Read it through; it's a wonderful prayer). Then he tasted a bit of cheap wine which someone put to his lips, but did not drink. He cried out clearly, in the madness of that afternoon which we call "good" Friday, that his work was finished: "It is consummated!" (John 19:30) Then he breathed forth his last breath, giving his soul back into his Father's hands: "Father, into your hands I commend my spirit." (Luke 23:46)

Can we hope to do more? Can we hope to do as much? Not saving the world, of course, just finishing our work.

On second thought, what is our work if it is not saving the world, in union with the only Savior?

–30–

DEATH THE LOSER IN A DUEL WITH LIFE

There was a time, at the dawn of the world, when the Lord God walked in the garden in the cool of the day. But Adam, the man in the story, hid himself among the trees. "Where are you?" the Lord called to him, and Adam answered, "I heard you in the garden and I was afraid because I was naked [Adam refers here to his loss of holiness], and I hid." (Genesis 3:10)

Ages later, there was another garden and another Man. This Man did not hide. He who had said to Lazarus, "Come forth!" himself emerged from the tomb that held him and stood in the light of day. Unlike Adam, he was neither naked nor ashamed. No, this Jesus, son of Joseph the carpenter, as was supposed, was clothed in the many-colored coat of glory which his heavenly Father had given him as a reward for his obedience. In the splendor of his risen body he rivaled the sunlight. The crucified Jesus, now made Lord and Messia, stood forth and said, like Moses at the burning bush, "Here I am" (Exodus 3:4), and like Isaia in the temple, "Lo, here am I, send me." (Isaia 6:8) He stood ready, in other words, to sanctify the world.

Unlike Jesus, Lord and Christ, man often tries to run out on his duties. In an old legend from Catalonia in Spain, we hear how the tiny hero, Padre Pantufet, got lost in the country one day. A kindly ox swallowed him to protect him. When Pantufet heard his parents calling, "Where are you?" he replied, "I am in the belly of the ox where it does not snow and it does not rain." What Pantufet did was run away from life. He made himself as he had been before he was born, in his mother's womb.

The prophet Jona ran away from responsibility in the same

way. He didn't want to do the job God had chosen for him: preach to the men of Nineveh. As he fled in fear, a whale swallowed him up. But his luck didn't last. He was thrown up on the shore and had to go to Nineveh anyway. That is the way it is when you oppose God. There's no place to hide.

Jesus knew the Jona story well. In referring to it, he used it as a sign of himself. "Just as Jona spent three days and three nights in the belly of the sea monster, so the Son of Man will spend three days and three nights in the heart of the earth." (Matthew 12:40) But Jesus did not hide in the heart of the earth. Even in death he was active, "going in the Spirit to bring the Good News to the spirits who were in prison [limbo]." (I Peter 3:19) He did not run, ostrich-like, to a resting place in a cool tomb. No, he went to limbo to free the fathers of Israel. Having done his work there, he came forth to press his advantage over death and hell, both of which he had conquered. He had a further work to do, and so he rose up to do it.

It was a strange war that Jesus had been through. As the poet, Francis Thompson, explains: "The slain had the gain and the victor had the rout." A smashing victory for Christ the "loser," while Satan, the "winner," was utterly defeated.

Jesus Christ got his scars "as they wounded all his brow, and they smote him through the side." But because he won his wounds in overthrowing Satan, the prince of this world, the Father gave him "titles that are high—'King of Kings!' are the words, 'Lord of Lords!'" During the Easter Vigil this year, you may remember, we prayed, "By his wounds holy and glorious may he preserve us who is Christ the Lord."

That is the basic message of the resurrection. We look for protection at the hands—the blood-red hands—of Christ, the one who did not run away.

Living in the twentieth century, as we've remarked before, is a far from easy business. All about us there's the attitude that no one is to blame for his own carelessness, his own ignorance, his own wrongdoing. "I blacked out," says the murderer or the rapist, meaning, "I got into one of those passionate rages I've been flying into since I was a kid." The rest of that statement ought to run, "No one ever stopped me before. What's this judge trying to do to me now?"

Another favorite modern trick is the hit-and-run performance. It happens every day in manslaughter cases. Even creasing someone's fender in a parking lot and driving off is not uncommon. "My brake slipped," is another way of saying, "My sense of decency—which was never very firm—slipped."

This is the era of the best machine-made products, installed by the sloppiest workmanship, in human history; it is the age of firing people by mail or through a secretary because bosses can't look them in the eye and give reasons; it is the era when people get more exercise passing the buck than they do walking. Sometimes it seems that the words that ought to be inscribed on one side of the great seal of the U.S. are, "Am I my brother's keeper?" and on the other, "The woman gave me the fruit . . . and I ate." We are fast becoming a nation of quitters, people who will do anything under the sun sooner than follow through on the consequences of their own actions.

Jesus of Nazareth had a task to finish and *he finished it.* His vocation was to be perfectly obedient to his Father's will, even though it meant his death on a cross. He answered this call, never looking to left or right. In spite of the cruelty of evil and thoughtless men, he continued to say to his Father what Satan could not say: "I will serve." When Saint Paul was speaking of this perfect obedience which led to Jesus' humiliation and death, he said, "That is why God has exalted him and given him the name above all names, so that at the name 'Jesus' everyone in heaven, on earth and beneath the earth should bend their knee and publicly acknowledge to the glory of God the Father that Jesus Christ is Lord." (Philippians 2:9–11)

Let us look at some of the events that led to the acknowledgment and praise of the Lordship of Christ on the morning he rose from the dead. First, several good women who had been his close friends in life (there were three, says Mark;

Luke adds a fourth name, but all mention Mary Magdalene as being one of them) went to his tomb early in the morning while it was still dark. They had assisted at his hasty burial before sundown on Friday night. Now they went back armed with many pounds of spices and ointments. The Jews didn't embalm as the Egyptians did, but they used sweet-smelling spices and ointments to lessen the odor of decay. The process of decay would have made steady progress in the nearly forty hours since Jesus' death. At least, it was natural for the women to think so.

When they got to the garden, the huge stone was rolled away from the door of the cave-like tomb. All their worry about how they would get into the outer chamber of the tomb was needless. The stone was already moved—by an earthquake, Saint Matthew says. (Matthew 28:2)

The *details* in the four accounts of the gospel differ in describing what the women found, just as they differ in the case of the Last Supper, or indeed almost any incident reported about Jesus. But the various accounts are quite alike in the *main lines* of the story, as they always are.

The women were terrified at finding the tomb unexpectedly open. They bent low and entered through the small door. Their first discovery was that there was no corpse of Jesus on the sandstone slab where they had laid it. They then discovered a youth (two of them, says Luke), with the appearance of a heavenly messenger, in the tomb. The messenger said to them, quite simply, "He is risen. He is not here." (Mark 16:6) By this time, the women were nearly petrified with fright. They bowed their faces to the ground so as not to have to look at the dazzling garments of the stranger who informed them. (Luke 24:4–5)

The mysterious youth (or "angel," as Saint Matthew calls him) assured the women not to be afraid: "For I know that you seek Jesus, who was crucified." (Matthew 28:5) Then, having showed them clearly that his body was not to be found, he directed them to report the event to the disciples. More than that, they were to meet him, the young man said, in Galilee—the scene of Jesus' prophecy that he would be crucified and on the third day rise. (Mark 16:7; Luke 24:6–7)

The women left the tomb area in a joyous state, but also trembling with "fear"—awe, actually, or dread—at how close the mystery of God had come to them. Off they went to report their breathtaking news to the Eleven and all the rest.

During his life, our Lord had told his disciples clearly that he would rise from the dead after his treatment at the hands of sinful men. In spite of this, the "tale seemed to them to be nonsense and they did not believe the women." (Luke 24:11) Two of them ran to the tomb to check for themselves, Peter and another. They stooped low to enter it and found the linen gravecloths neatly folded there. Of Jesus they saw nothing. They believed the evidence of their senses, namely that the tomb was, in fact, empty. But, says the fourth gospel, "They had not as yet understood the Scripture text which says that he must rise from the dead. The disciples then left from home." (John 20:9–10)

Up to this point, the account of Christ's rising up from the dead is a kind of mystery story. Frank Morison has written a serious book about the events of Easter morning which catches this spirit perfectly. He calls it *Who Moved the Stone?*

Jesus did not rise from death to provide us with a puzzle, however. He meant to give us life—to make us alive in him. You best get the idea of this in the meeting between the risen Jesus and Mary Magdalene in the garden. (John 20:11–18) She sees him but does not know him, for she is weeping. Taking him for a groundskeeper, she pleads for Jesus' body, if he should have it. Our Lord then calls her by name. To his "Mary," she answers "Rabboni—my Master." This is the moment that matters: the instant of recognition. After it, but only after it, she can say, "I have seen the Lord!"

Those are the events of the first Easter morning. They are an *end* and a *beginning*. An end to grief, to death, to sin that caused the Master's death; a beginning of glory and new life. Notice this, though. As a rumor or report, the resurrection story is meaningless. It signifies nothing to Peter and the other disciples at this point. They have only heard about it. They neither believe nor disbelieve it. They are unchanged.

Mary, however, has seen the risen Jesus, spoken to him. For her, everything is different now. She has acknowledged him as Lord and Master, and this commitment affects her whole way of living.

That is the way it is with you and me. We either know *about* Christ's resurrection, or we *know* it. Our moment of clear recognition of the person of the risen Christ is chiefly in the eucharist. But, we also meet him when we perform any act of love, for his eucharistic body is the sign of love.

He has called out to you: "Joe," "Helen," "Manuel." Have you heard him? Enough to say, "Master!"?

-31-

THE FORTY DAYS AND THE PASCHAL FAITH

In the first chapter of this book, we spoke of the strong faith in him that Jesus' disciples had when they first began to proclaim his death and resurrection to the crowds in Jerusalem. By that time, Jesus' followers believed two great things about him: that he was Lord, a title that had the ring of "God" to the pious Jew, and that he was Christ, Israel's Messia. The forward movement of the four accounts of the gospel describes the slow progress Jesus had in getting the seeds of these two ideas across to his friends. Actually, the gospel makes it clear that they didn't really succeed in understanding these ideas during his lifetime.

The unfolding of the great mystery of who he was, and the work of saving men that the Father had sent him to do, had to be gone about slowly, very slowly. The disciples' "dullness of heart" (we would call it their "stupidity" or "resistance") got in the way. It was only the Holy Spirit's coming down on the Twelve that gave them the understanding, the courage and the desire to spread the good news (the meaning of the word "gospel") about Christ. The power they received when the Holy Spirit came on them sent them out to be Christ's witnesses in Jerusalem, all Judea and Samaria, and even to the very ends of the earth. (Read Acts 1:7–8).

Yet there was one period in the Savior's earthly stay that greatly helped prepare his followers' hearts for the spread of the gospel. It was, of course, the time of his risen life, the period between his resurrection, and his ascension into heaven. When we spoke in the preceding chapter of Jesus' coming forth from the tomb, we did not describe how it happened. We only spoke of what he said and did *after* he had risen. That is because the gospel does not describe his resurrection as it takes place, but as something that has just *taken* place. There is, in other words, no gospel account of the "rising Christ," but only one of the "risen Christ."

Saint Matthew does tell us that when Jesus sent his disciples to bring word to his brethren to set out for Galilee (a good distance from Jerusalem), some of the guards over Jesus' tomb came into the city to report to the chief priests all that had happened. (Matthew 28:11–15) The leaders bribed the guards to say that Jesus' body had been stolen while they were sleeping. This is the story you hear in Jerusalem "even to the present day," Saint Matthew said, when he wrote his account of the gospel.

But aside from the guards and their employers, who suspect something, the only people who we are sure know about Jesus' risen life are his friends who come to believe in it. He gives them courage by appearing to them and teaching them about the kingdom of God "throughout forty days." (Acts 1:3) He showed himself alive to them, after his passion, "giving many conclusive proofs," says Saint Luke, that he is alive. (Acts 1:3)

The Church's belief in Christ's death and resurrection is known as "the paschal faith." The Church has always had this belief, from the time she first came to be the Church. The roots of this faith are described in the period between the first Easter and the first Pentecost. During this time, that is to say up to his ascension, the Twelve on whom the Spirit descended (Acts 1:13) are visited by Jesus from time to time. He wants to plant this faith deep in their hearts. *Paschal* is a word that comes from the Greek word for *Passover*. Here it means the faith of Christians that Jesus Christ, our passover Lamb, has not only been sacrificed, but has also been raised up in glory. *Paschal faith is the faith of Christians in the fact of the resurrection.*

We really ought to examine the appearances of the Lord to his friends, one by one, so that we'll know what "conclusive proofs" of his resurrection he gave them. *You and I must have the faith in him as the risen, glorious Christ that the Church has.* If we don't, then we will go through life with only a half-hearted conviction of the "resurrection of the body and life everlasting" which we say we believe, in the Apostles' Creed. Life is hard enough. Not having a clear goal in sight can make it unbearable. "Going-to-heaven-when-I-die" may suit some people, but it is hardly definite enough to suit the Christian.

No sir! The Christian's *complete* faith is that he will be raised up in the glory of a risen body because Christ has first been raised up in glory. "If Christ has not been raised," Saint Paul says, "your faith is groundless." (I Corinthians 15:17) He means that the faith of the Church is that Christ's resurrection is going to be the cause of yours and mine. If our Lord's resurrection didn't take place, Saint Paul says quite logically, we had better look into *that*, for it would mean that our bodies are going to lie in the earth forever.

If Christ didn't rise from the dead, in other words, we actually have nothing to hope for. Living on as a "soul" for all eternity won't do. That state is only a temporary one, to last until Christ returns to earth in glory and raises up the dead. The Church has never believed that living on as a "soul" would be man's final end, because God loves us the way he made us, and that means body and soul. If he means to bring us to himself, he will surely do it by giving us a come-as-you-are invitation. We are to come, not as angels nor as spooks, but as human beings, body and soul. (Read Chapter 15 of Saint Paul's first letter to the Christians at Corinth. It will help you to know clearly what Catholics believe about life after death).

Jesus' first visit that we are told about, after the early morning ones that we examined in the last chapter, took place "that very day" (Luke 24:13), the day Jesus rose from the dead. Saint Mark mentions very briefly that the Lord appeared "in another form" to two disciples as they went into the country (Mark 16:12), but Saint Luke describes it at length.

Remember, that Sunday was no sacred day in those times, let alone Easter day, as it is for us now. The great Passover Sabbath was ended and it was a business-as-usual morning.

Even though the Jews could not eat yeast for a week, in remembrance of their deliverance from slavery in Egypt, they did resume their ordinary tasks. Many of the pilgrims to Jerusalem broke camp, so to say, and went home that morning. Two men who had begun to believe in Jesus were making their way, downcast, to the town of Emmaus, seven miles from Jerusalem, when they were joined by a stranger. They had been talking about the hopes they had placed in Jesus of Nazareth, which had all been crushed by his death.

When the stranger expressed his ignorance of these facts they were surprised. They patiently explained to him that Jesus was a prophet, "mighty in deed and word in the eyes of God and the mass of the people." They went on to say: "We had hoped He might be the man destined to redeem Israel." But, alas, his death had happened three days ago, so now they had nothing to hope for. They *had* heard a story of an empty tomb and a vision of angels to some women (Luke 24:22–24), but they weren't putting much stock in it. They told the stranger that while the empty tomb was evidently a fact, the women had not seen Jesus in person.

At this point, Jesus, who was the stranger (they did not realize this because "their eyes were prevented from recognizing Him," Luke 24:16), finally broke in. He called them dull, and told them they were slow to understand what the prophets had said whenever the prophets' message had to do with the Messia and suffering. "Was it not necessary," he asked, "for the Messia to undergo these sufferings and *thus* enter into his glory?" Time and again, you see, Jesus recalled the Suffering Servant of the Lord, meaning himself. Then he carefully went through the main parts of Israel's holy books with them, from Moses through all the prophets, "explaining the passages which referred to himself in every part of the scriptures." (Luke 24:27)

When he rose to go, they begged him to stay with them for the evening meal. As he took bread, he said the blessing over it, broke it and offered it to them (the very words used to describe his action at the Last Supper). Then, "their eyes were opened and they recognized him . . . in the breaking of bread." (Luke 24:31, 35) But he vanished from their sight.

The two men raced back to Jerusalem with their news, only to be told that Peter had also seen the Lord. After that, the appearances of Jesus began to multiply. On "that same day, the first of the week" (John 20:19–23), Jesus came to them behind closed doors while the apostle Thomas was absent. He gave them the gift of his peace, and then the gift of the Holy Spirit. As the Father had sent him into the world, so Jesus sent his disciples. He gave them power in the Spirit to forgive or not to forgive sins. This shouldn't surprise us. The whole purpose of his dying and rising was "the forgiveness of sins," as the Apostles' Creed says. Now the work is done, and he is able to give this gift.

Saint Luke tells the story of Jesus breaking in on his startled and panic-stricken friends on the night the two Emmaus disciples returned to Jerusalem. (Luke 24:36–43) He asked for food while he was with them, and ate some broiled fish and a honeycomb. His first efforts to show them he was not a ghost were not proving successful, even though he told them to examine his hands and feet: "Feel me and convince yourselves," are Jesus' words. (Luke 24:39) The disbelief continued, however, and the Lord scolded them for it. (Mark 16:14)

Saint John is the one who tells the famous story of "doubting Thomas." Jesus came to visit his friends one week to the day after his resurrection. Thomas missed him the first time, and he said later, "Unless I see in his hands the print of the nails, and put my finger into the place of the nails, and my hand into his side, I will not believe." (John 20:25) That is exactly what Jesus made him do, however, and Thomas responded in awe and amazement: "My Lord and my God!"

Perhaps the most attractive account of an appearance of Christ is one given by Saint John. (John 21:1–3) He tells how seven of the Twelve had gone back to Galilee and taken up their work again. They were fishing on their familiar lake—probably wondering what the marvelous events they had witnessed could mean—when Jesus joined them at the lakeshore. He cooked a breakfast of fish and bread for them. On this occasion, the Lord gave Peter the special responsibility of taking care of his flock. He did this by putting to him the question "Do you love me?" three times. Lambs and sheep, the Master said, all need feeding, even though this work of feeding them may end by Peter's being dragged off to death. (John 21:19)

The mysteries of Christ's resurrection and of his ascent to his Father are joined in one—the mystery of his "glory." Even though the proofs of the mystery of his glory are several, and, in Saint Luke's phrase, the time of them forty days, the glorification of Jesus by the Father remains a single mystery. The mystery of Jesus' glory should mean a lot to us. This is the great sign that death is not final. This shows us that the body which causes us so such trouble in life, with its needs and demands, is meant to end in an entirely different state from the one it has now. It is meant to end in *glory*.

Jesus controlled his Body by his thoughts and his obedient will. He made it his servant, not his master. The result? No grave could hold him, because he did *perfectly*—in soul and body—what was required of him.

Think of that the next time there's a rebellion going on inside of you. There is the stinking decay of the tomb—a sign of hell, because sin causes death—and there is the glory of the man who rises with Christ.

That's the choice. For a whole lifetime you have to make that choice—afresh, each day.

-32-

JESUS SENDS ANOTHER TO SUSTAIN US

Almost every one knows who the Quakers are, that religious Society of Friends to which William Penn belonged. They were founded by George Fox, a pious young Englishman of the 1600's, as a "peculiar people" (different, that is) who lived simply, as the gospel demanded. They were called "in scorn by their detractors Quakers," Fox wrote, because when the Spirit of God or Inner Light spoke to their spirit during a "meeting" they quaked all over. The Shakers are a similar group. (Have you heard of Shaker Heights, Ohio, named for them?) Their real name is "The United Society of Believers in Christ's Second Appearing," but because they shook "in holy expectation before the Lord," people called them Shakers.

Holy Rollers get their name in the same way. So do the "jumper Churches" of the U.S. southland and the islands of the Caribbean. The largest bodies of this sort are the many Pentecostal Churches, some of which are entitled "Assemblies of God." A common sign to be seen in U.S. cities where Puerto Rican and other Spanish-speaking Americans live is one in the form of a cross bearing the words *Iglesia Pentecostal*–Pentecostal Church. People who know a lot about the growth of religious bodies say that these groups (and the Jehovah's Witnesses, who say they aren't a church) are likely to comprise the largest totals of non-Catholic Christians in a a hundred years–more numerous than all the Protestants in the world–depending on what happens in Latin America.

It is important to bring this matter up because these believers have a firm grasp on one great Catholic principle at least, namely that the Spirit of God dwells in the Church. They are sound as can be on that, though they may not be so firm on other mysteries of faith. We must try to learn from them. If anyone should say to you, "Where do you Catholics get the right to claim that you are the Church of Jesus Christ?", a good *first* answer would be: "We are a family of charity in whom the Holy Spirit dwells." Later we might tell our questioner certain other things, for example, how the eucharist can be celebrated with a perfect love only where there is a bishop who has complete or Catholic faith; how the Church is composed of all those "made into one" by eucharists like those celebrated in a Catholic "household" (the Greek word is *diocese*) by a bishop or one of his priests, and so on. But the first thing we should say is: "Ours is the faith of Jesus Christ because the Holy Spirit lives in our midst."

What underlies every chapter in this book is the message of God to men—and that is a serious business. Not a heavy business. Not somber or dull, but joyous. Lively in fact. Nonetheless, a matter of life and death. This message is a Word spoken by God to men in the person of Jesus Christ, and kept alive in our hearts by the Spirit whom he sends from the Father.

There is a possibility you may not have known until reading these chapters, and the parts of the Bible they send you to, how full of mystery Jesus the Lord is. That he is the Son of God and the second person of the blessed Trinity you knew. God has taught this and Catholics believe it. You are a Catholic (well—many who read this are), and you believe it. Simple as ABC, in a way. It is only when you begin to look into the gospels that you see how much lies beneath the statement: "Jesus Christ is true God and true man." The closer you examine the words and actions of this mysterious Person the better you understand him. At the same time, however, you become less sure of yourself and of the tidy little mental picture you had of the Savior up till now.

Close study of the New Testament shows that he was much more fully human than we had supposed, and also much more divine. A better way to express it would be to say that his divine-humanness (or God-man-ness) escapes us farther and farther, the more we get to know him. God reveals, unfolds, the mystery of himself in Christ. As he does so, something of the hiddenness of God becomes known to us. He is terribly near to us, yet we will never understand him. An infinity sets us apart from him, yet he is our familiar friend. All this grows clearer as we reflect on Jesus' words: "Philip . . . he who sees me sees the Father." (John 14:9)

This should have been a hard book to get through, if you struggled to know the mysteriousness and the friendship of Jesus. If it were easy, it wouldn't have been him at all you were confronting, but only some caricature. His friendship is hard won. The splendor of God himself shines out of those eyes, not that of a Colonel Glenn or a Dr. Tom Dooley. Moreover, it is impossible to know Jesus unless the strong Counselor whom he sends us from the Father gives us light and understanding. If a man can't even say the name "Jesus" in faith without the Holy Spirit's help (so Paul says in I Corinthians 12:3), how can he take in the whole *person* of the Lord apart from this help? It is quite impossible, obviously. Something that is very easy, on the other hand, is to study about Jesus on a shallow level and then—without much effort and without the Holy Spirit's guidance—to say that we "know" the Lord. All we would be knowing in that case is our own puny mental image of him. That picture is an easy one to take in because it is so much like us and so much unlike him.

The whole idea of sacred art can be of great help here. Do you know why the Greek Christians of old used to show Christ with coal-black eyes, a nose like a hawk's beak, and hair the color of tar? Was it because they couldn't paint, or set mosaic-tile, any better than that? Nothing of the sort. They knew they were representing someone who was the great Mystery of God, and that if they portrayed an ordinary man whom you could take in at a glance they had failed in their task.

But the Jesus who is, the Lord of the New Covenant, is nothing like an image of ourselves. "Then He turned around, and looked full on Peter." (Luke 22:61) "Here He changed His appearance before their eyes . . . then a cloud formed and enveloped them, and a voice rang out in the cloud: 'This is my beloved Son. Listen to Him!'" (Mark 9:3,8) "At this very moment (Stephen speaks), I see the skies opened and the Son of Man standing at the right hand of God." (Acts 7:56) "I saw heaven opened. I saw a white horse, and its rider is called Faithful and True . . . His eyes are like a flame of fire . . . He is clothed in a garment sprinkled with blood, and his name is 'The Word of God' . . . He will rule them with an iron rod . . . on his robe is his name inscribed, 'King of Kings and Lord of Lords.'" (Apocalypse 19:11–16)

As this brief volume draws to a close, we ought to be asking ourselves what impact our faith in Jesus Christ is having on those who know us. Can they tell, for example, that the beloved Son of the Father is our intimate friend? That we willingly serve the faithful and true one who is King of Kings and Lord of Lords? Often, it seems, our acquaintances cannot so much as guess this. The friends of Jesus huddle together like frightened sheep, hoping no one will bring up the embarrassing question of religion, particularly *their* religion. They follow the Lamb of God, all right. The Rider on a white horse with eyes like a flame of fire they don't know very well.

Browse in the Acts of the Apostles for a bit to see how the men who first preached about Jesus conducted themselves. They did many wonders and signs (Acts 2:43); they taught the people, and proclaimed in the case of Jesus' resurrection from the dead (4:2); they said they could not keep from speaking of what they had seen and heard. (4:20) Why such boldness on their parts? Because they were filled with the Holy Spirit! (See Acts 2:4; 4:31; 6:5; 8:29; 9:17; 10:44; 13:9). They rejoiced that they had been counted worthy to suffer disgrace for the name of Jesus. Never for a single day did they cease teaching and preaching the good news about him. (5:41–42) You couldn't shut them up.

When St. Paul went spreading the good news he came to Ephesus where he found a group of believers. They had been baptized in the name of the Lord Jesus but had never heard of the Holy Spirit! Paul laid his hands on them, and immediately the Spirit came on them in full measure. (Acts 19:1–7)

If you had to describe the life of the infant Church, no phrase would do it better than to say that it was a community impelled and ruled by the Holy Spirit. It had to be that way, of course, if it really was Christ's Church. "Unless I depart," he had said, "the Advocate will not come to you." (John 16:7) "When the Spirit of truth has come, he will conduct you through the whole range of truth." (V. 13) "He will teach you everything, and refresh your memory on everything I have told you." (John 14:26)

Almost every reader of this book has been confirmed, which means you have the gift of the Holy Spirit. All through these pages you have been reading the good news about Jesus Christ in whom you have been saved. You must let that sacrament do its work in you now. Let the Holy Ghost refresh your memories on all you have learned. You and your family and your friends, all confirmed in the Spirit, must be welded by Him into a holy community which will make men say: "They *have* to be the Church of Jesus Christ. They have the Spirit of Jesus (Acts 16:7), don't they—the Spirit of truth and love?"

It isn't they alone who live. It's—well, actually, it's *Christ* who lives in them.

ECHO BOOKS

ECHO BOOKS are a series of popularly written paperbound books of Catholic interest for the modern reader. All areas of literature are to be represented in the series—fiction, non-fiction, biography, autobiography, Church history, the Bible, lives of great Catholics, Church doctrine, and works of a spiritual nature. The aim of ECHO BOOKS is to offer worthwhile books of Catholic appeal that will provide wholesome, informative, entertaining, and inspirational reading in inexpensive paperbound editions.

ECHO BOOKS was chosen as the name of the series as it is our hope that these books will echo, through popular literature, the word of God and the teachings of the Catholic Church.

We welcome the comments and suggestions of ECHO BOOKS readers at all times. A circular describing all the ECHO BOOKS available may be obtained from your nearest bookseller or directly from the publisher.